ITV's Ki

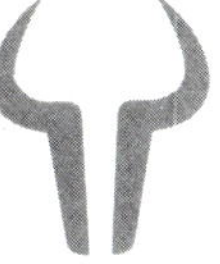

ITV's Kitchen Garden

Growing and Cooking Fruit and Vegetables

Keith Fordyce and Claire Rayner

Based on the Thames Television series
produced by George Sawford

Stanley Paul, London

Acknowledgement
Mr Barker (Royal Horticultural Society, Wisley) for supplying fruit for the jacket photograph.

Stanley Paul & Co Ltd
3 Fitzroy Square, London W 1 P 6 J D

An imprint of the Hutchinson Publishing Group

London Melbourne Sydney Auckland
Wellington Johannesburg and agencies throughout the world

In association with Independent Television Books

First published 1978

Filmset in Univers Light by Newgate Press Ltd, London
Printed in Great Britain by The Anchor Press Ltd
and bound by Wm Brendon & Son Ltd,
both of Tiptree, Essex

ISBN 0 09 132780 6 (cased)
0 09 132781 4 (paperback)

The vegetable sections of the book and the vegetable recipes have previously been published by Independent Television Books for direct mail only.

Contents

Introduction

Writing this book has been a lot harder than recording the television series. It seems to be so much easier to show someone how something should be done rather than to explain it in words. But I hope you will find the following chapters helpful as an *aide-mémoire* when you set about growing your own fruit and vegetables. Like so many other occupations, gardening is one that gets easier with experience – and you can pack a tremendous lot of experience into just one growing season. But unlike many other occupations if you get it wrong the first time there is always next year, and you can start all over again, benefiting from your mistakes.

Don't be put off if some of the procedures for cultivation described in this book seem difficult or complicated. It always turns out a lot simpler when you are actually doing the job, as opposed to when you are reading about it. You may find it encouraging to remember that I myself am no expert, just an amateur who enjoys some of the work (let's be honest) and all of the results. Especially when Claire Rayner has turned those results into a tasty and original dish. I have been given lots of valuable advice by Fred Potter and Jim Smith of Suttons Seeds and Harry Barker and Bertie Doe of the Royal Horticultural Society, and I am very grateful to them for their patience and understanding. What I have tried to do is to pass on their advice in a basic form that will be easy to understand.

A good seed catalogue is a mine of information – a gardener's 'bible' that not only helps with the seasonal work but also gives great pleasure when you feel like a spot of arm-chair gardening in frozen January. If you feel you need much more detail about growing a particular crop, there is of course a wide range of specialist books on every aspect of gardening to be had from a bookshop or your public library. Joining a local horticultural society is also a good idea. As well as giving you a chance to obtain discounts on some products and implements this will put you in earshot of the all-important 'know-how' that nearly all gardeners are only too keen to pass on.

In the following chapters I have suggested times for sowing and transplanting, but these are intended only as a rough guide. Sowing depends very much on the type of soil you have in your garden and on the weather conditions in any particular season. Adjustments need to be made to allow for these varying conditions, but this is something you can only judge for yourself – unless, that is, you can call on the advice of a friend or neighbour who is an experienced gardener. For instance, when it comes to sowing seeds, the depth of the drill will vary quite a lot according to the soil. (The general rule is to sow in a shallow drill when the soil is on the heavy side and a little deeper if the soil is light.)

Vegetable growing is a rewarding and satisfying pastime. Some hard work is involved, but surprisingly little. In the first part of this book you will find out how to cut hard work to a minimum, and to harvest some succulent vegetables that will have cost you relatively little to produce. The next section deals with the art of growing fruit, and while the advice given in Chapter 2 is useful for gardeners generally, there is more specific information directed at the fruit grower in Chapters 8–14.

Growing vegetables

Glossary

Bed out: To plant a seedling into its final growing place.

Brassicas: The word used to describe the cabbage family and some roots such as swedes and turnips.

Calomel: A chemical usually used as a 4 per cent compound in a dust to stop club root in brassicas, carrot root fly, etc.

Compost: Rotting vegetation used to fertilize the soil, or a special soil mixture for raising seeds and seedlings.

Dibber: A pointed piece of wood used to make a hole for tubers or seedlings.

Drill: A furrow made in the ground, which can be either V-shaped or flat-bottomed, in which to sow seeds.

Fertilizer: Plant food put into soil to replace that used up by previous crops.

Haulm: The foliage of potatoes, runner beans and some other plants.

Humus: Decayed vegetable matter used to enrich the soil.

Inorganic fertilizer: Artificial fertilizer as opposed to organic fertilizer, quicker acting than organic fertilizer.

Manure: Decomposed animal or vegetable matter used as a soil nutrient.

Nitrogenous: Containing nitrogen, one of the most important requirements for plant growth.

Organic fertilizer: A fertilizer consisting of decomposed animal matter, e.g. horse manure, compost, etc.

Pinching out: Removing unwanted shoots from a plant.

Seedling: A young plant consisting only of the main stem and no side shoots.

Singling: To reduce a group of seedlings to one.

Sow: To put seeds into a suitable medium to start growth.

Spit: The depth of a spade, usually about 30 cm (12 in.).

Thinning: Removing some seedlings to enable those left in the soil to have room to grow.

Tilth: Soil broken down very finely with a rake or hoe for sowing seeds.

Transplant: To move a growing plant from one place to another, e.g. from pot to garden.

Truss: The stem of a plant that bears clusters of flowers or fruit.

Tubers: The name applied to the swollen roots of plants like potatoes or dahlias; these roots are a food store and produce shoots for the following year's growth.

1

Groundwork

In the spring a gardener's fancy lightly turns to thoughts of double spit digging, compost heaps, manure, and what he or she will be harvesting in June. When you get the urge to grow something, early spring is the time to start. Even if your sole contribution to the world of horticulture has been a saucer of mustard and cress at the Infants' School, don't be disheartened: vegetable growing is not as difficult as you may think.

Choosing the site

Our kitchen garden plot is 7 × 3 m (24 × 10 ft) – that is, about a quarter the size of the garden of the average semi-detached house – and on this plot you can grow thirty different crops, sufficient to supply most of the requirements of two people for a year. If you are growing for a larger family then increase the size of the plot and the number of vegetables accordingly. The site you choose should get as much sunlight as possible and should be sheltered from the prevailing winds. Do not make the mistake of putting your vegetable plants under the old oak tree, because nothing will thrive there. The young plants will simply race upwards in an attempt to reach the sunlight, and finally run to seed.

If your back garden is unsuitable, then why not consider the front? The neighbours may titter at your cabbage rows where the cabbage rose should be but it will be your turn to laugh in the early summer when the neighbours are paying the earth for their vegetables and yours are coming fresh and free. If neither front nor back garden is suitable, and you still want to grow something, don't despair; you can always apply for a council allotment instead. Be warned, though: there is a waiting list for allotments, particularly in the larger urban areas, so the earlier you apply the better. An allotment will cost you approximately 16p per week per rod. (A rod is just under 30 sq. m (35 sq. yd) – slightly larger than the kitchen garden plot.) Write to the parks and gardens department of your local council for an application form.

What to grow

In the following chapters you will read about some of the more popular vegetables such as cabbages and carrots, beans, beet and marrow, as well as some of the lesser-

Our kitchen garden vegetable plot

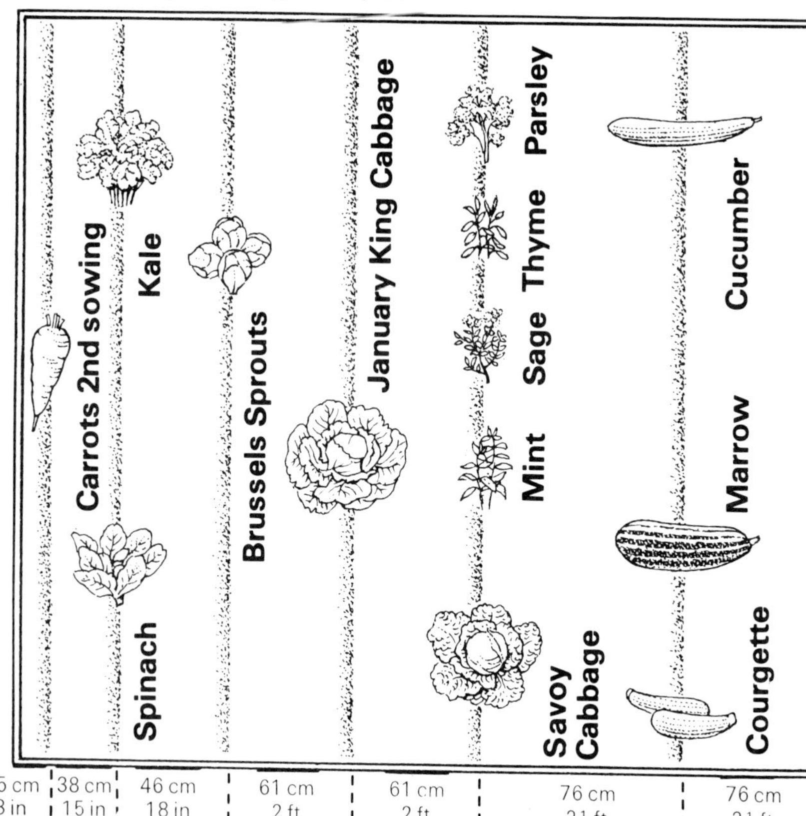

known, like salsify, kohl rabi, Chevriers Verts, and mangetout peas. What you grow is of course a matter of taste – a glorious bed of spinach may look impressive but it isn't much good if the kids can't stand the stuff! Another word of warning: don't be tempted to oversow. One courgette plant, for instance, should produce enough fruit for two people during the season, so unless you intend keeping the street in courgettes, don't plant a whole row of them. If you have seeds left over give them to your neighbour, or better still, buy Harvest Fresh variety. They are slightly more expensive but will keep until the following season.

Tools of the trade

Gardeners can spend a small fortune on tools and equipment, from the basic essentials to the more sophisticated

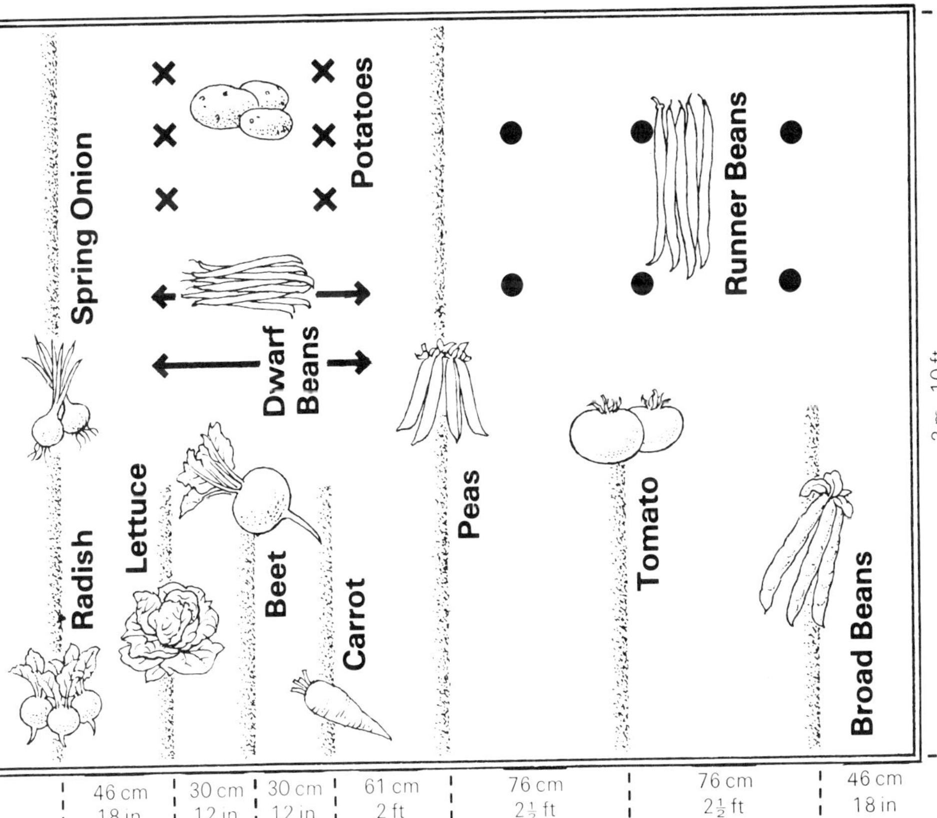

and the plain gimmicky. To start with, you will only need the basics: spade, fork, hoe, etc. As with many things, the most expensive are not always the best, so shop around for them. Try the sale rooms, the classified ads in the local paper, auctions of house contents and so on. Secondhand garden tools can often be of very good quality and usually they are relatively inexpensive.

Most households will already have a useful collection of tools, even if they have never been used for gardening! But for those just starting, here is a list of some of the more necessary implements.

Strong spade
Strong fork
Shovel
Trowel
Rake
Draw hoe: Used to make 'drills' (small, shallow trenches for planting beans, peas and smaller seeds)
Dutch hoe: Essential for keeping the plot free of weeds, and it takes the backache out of weeding
Small hand or onion hoe: Used for detailed work such as hoeing in between small young seedlings

Homemade tools

Three items that are useful and that can easily be made at home are a dibber, a measuring rod, and a wooden mallet.

The dibber is a round length of timber with a point at one end. A broken spade handle is ideal, or even a piece of broomstick. It is used for making small holes for bulbs, tubers and for seedlings when transplanting.

You will find a measuring rod is invaluable for measuring distances between rows and between individual plants. To make a measuring rod take a piece of 5×2.5 cm (2×1 in.) timber, smooth it off and paint it white. It can be any length you choose, but it is best to keep it to manageable proportions – roughly 2 m (6 ft) or so. On one side of your measuring rod mark off 15 cm (6 in.) lengths with heavier markings on every other 15 cm marking – that is, the 30 cm (12 in.) markings. Number the metres (or feet) to however

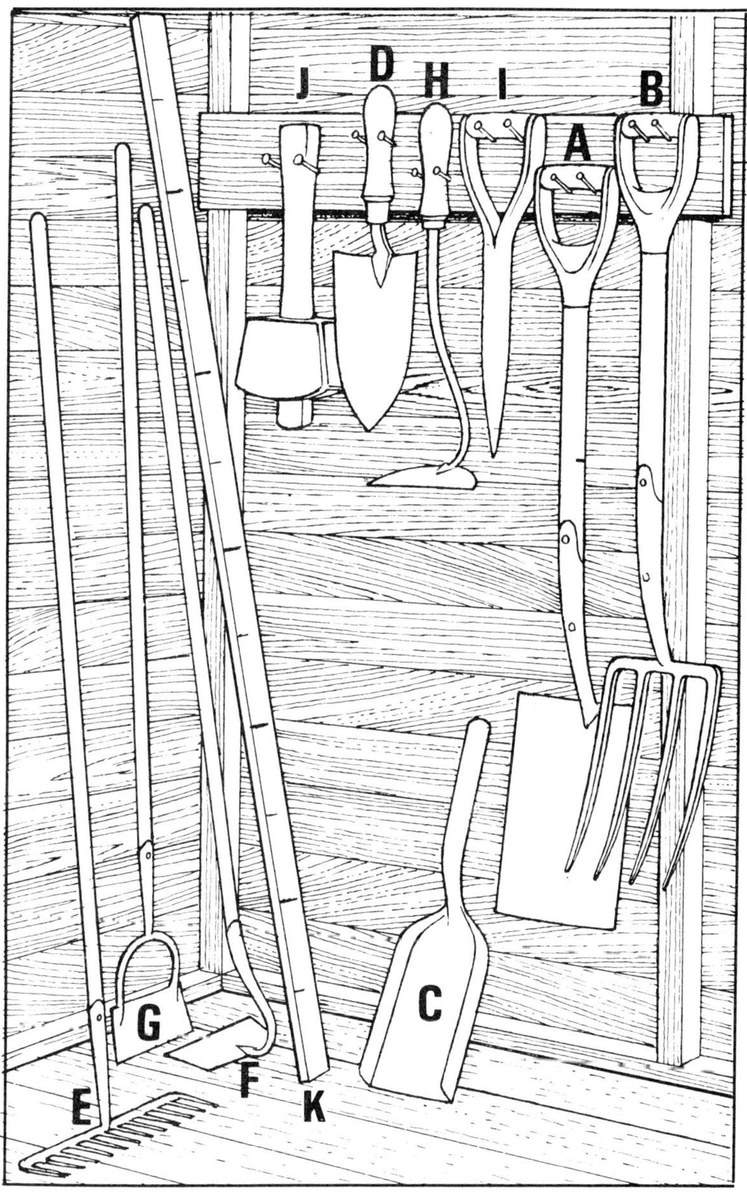

A *Strong spade*	D *Trowel*	G *Dutch hoe*	I *Dibber*
B *Strong fork*	E *Rake*	H *Small hand or onion hoe*	J *Mallet*
C *Shovel*	F *Draw hoe*		K *Measuring rod*

long your rod is. As an optional extra every third 15 cm (6 in.) can be marked 45 cm (18 in.) – this then gives you 15 cm (6 in.), 30 cm (12 in.) and 45 cm (18 in.) markings at a glance. Mark out 38 cm (15 in.) spacing on the reverse side of your rod and there you have all the measurements you will need for your plot in an instant.

A mallet is another useful implement. You will need a piece of hardwood about 38 cm (15 in.) long, and 7.5–10 cm (3–4 in.) square. Make a saw mark right round the wood, about 12.5 cm (5 in.) from the end. Shave down this short end to a handsize grip, and there you have a made-to-measure mallet. Very useful for driving in canes, stakes and line stumps, etc.

There are many more tools that you may find useful, but for the moment those already mentioned will be all you need for growing vegetables. See Chapter 9 for the additional tools needed for growing fruit.

Plant food

The ideal food for plants is manure (except where you are going to plant root crops in the first year). But manure does have disadvantages: farmyard manure is very difficult to come by, and the neighbours may well object to a steaming heap of horse dung over the fence as they sit down to their tea. A gardening friend of mine tells me his vegetables thrive on elephant dung which he gets from a nearby safari park, but then he has very understanding neighbours . . . they are giraffes! However, we don't all live next door to the zoo or the local riding stables, so there has to be an alternative to manure. The most readily available is garden peat used with an inorganic fertilizer. 'Hoof and Horn' and 'Bonemeal' are both good and easily obtainable fertilizers. But homemade compost is in many ways the best, and is certainly the cheapest and most satisfying since it is made from refuse and waste.

Compost

You will need a container for your compost to prevent it spilling all over the garden. Mark out a square, roughly

150 cm (5 ft). Place posts at each corner, and stretch some wire netting between the posts. Old fencing will do just as well, instead of netting, or you could even use an old packing case, open at the bottom, although this would obviously be smaller than the measurements given above. It is simply a matter of making four walls to contain your compost. Remember not to put the compost heap near to your house or near to the neighbours, because it will tend to smell and won't look very pretty either.

Once you have a four-walled frame you can begin to make your compost. Start the heap with a layer of straw or grass mowings, provided of course that the grass has not previously been treated with a weedkiller. Then simply pile in garden and kitchen refuse – not just vegetable peelings, but the stuff you scrape off the plates as well, until it is about 30 cm (12 in.) deep. Add another layer of straw or grass mowings and some sulphate of ammonia, or one of the proprietary brands of compost accelerator; then more waste up to about 30 cm (12 in.) deep, followed by another layer of straw or grass mowings and a sprinkling of sulphate of ammonia. Turn the compost over at four-week intervals and leave the rest to nature. In a few months you will have a heap of delicious humus – the plants will find it delicious even if you don't.

The compost may take a little longer to mature in the winter months because it likes warmth, so from October through to May keep your compost covered by old sacks. An occasional watering during very dry periods will also assist decomposition.

Fertilizer

The feeding of plants with fertilizer is not absolutely essential. Provided you have prepared your soil well at the beginning of the season, the plants should get all they need from the soil. It may be necessary to feed some crops, though, if they don't appear to be doing particularly well. Plants should certainly not be overfed. A top dressing of fertilizer should be all that is needed. Ideally, the fertilizer should be applied when the ground is moist, as feeding in the middle of a dry spell can cause scorching of the roots. As for quantity, a handful of fertilizer scattered along either side of a 150 cm (5 ft) row should be all that is necessary. Hoe the fertilizer in with the dutch hoe.

Containers

In the following pages I shall recommend various kinds of pots and containers differing in shape and size according to their intended use. Clay and plastic pots can, of course, be used over and over again, but they are more expensive to buy initially. Which reminds me: when you are 'tapping out' a plant from a pot ready to put it into the garden, do exercise a little delicacy. Hold the pot upside down with your fingers restraining the plant and the soil and then gently tap the rim of the pot (not the base) until the plant and soil become dislodged. It is that gentle tap that counts – otherwise you may end up with an awful lot of chipped, cracked or broken pots! 'Pots' made from black polythene are a lot cheaper but can be used only once. When a plant in this type of container is ready to go into the garden there is no need to remove it; just make sure there is a good split down both sides of the polythene and put the whole lot into the soil. The soil ball will then remain undisturbed.

Control of pests

Most plants suffer from pests of one sort or another, but thanks to the use of modern chemicals, these pests are more easily controlled than they were in Grandad's day, when blackfly could do nearly as much damage as Moses's plague of locusts. There are two main types of chemical spray in use. The first is sprayed directly on to the infestation. This has the same effect as squirting fly-spray on to a fly, attacking the cause of the trouble at the moment it occurs.

The second type is called systemic. With this type the chemical is absorbed by the foliage, and is therefore much slower acting. It can, however, be most useful since few people have the time to rush into the garden armed with a spray every time a greenfly is spotted. The systemic type of spray is also extremely useful for spraying plants before you go on holiday; though slower acting they are also longer lasting.

Always spray below the leaves as well as above, particularly with the first type of spray. This deals with insects hiding under the leaves.

Caution with sprays

Certain chemicals can be used on certain plants while being unsuitable for others. On a small plot this obviously presents problems. It is almost impossible to spray one crop on one small part of the plot and at the same time avoid adjacent crops, so you must in some way isolate the crop you are spraying. This can be done by covering all neighbouring plants with plastic sheeting or old plastic sacks while you spray the crop in need of treatment. Wash the plastic sacks after use, and of course wash your hands, mixing vessels, containers and sprayers very thoroughly. Finally, a most important word of warning. Keep all chemicals correctly and clearly labelled, keep their lids securely on and *keep them out of the reach of children.*

Spraying equipment

A number of types of sprayer are available, from the simple hand-operated pump, like an oversized scent spray, to the sophisticated pressurized back-packs. The simpler variety is quite adequate for the kitchen garden and should not cost more than £1.50. The chemicals for the spray may be a further £2.50. Three different types of spray should cover most pests and many diseases. These chemicals will make up to about 136 litres (30 gal.) of liquid and should last about two seasons.

If time is too limited to mix chemicals, you could use aerosols. They are more expensive than mix-it-yourself chemicals, but they are certainly effective.

When spraying, whether with hand spray, back-pack or aerosol, remember:

1. Read the instructions carefully.
2. Pick a mild and, if possible, windless day (your neighbour may not want his crops sprayed).
3. Cover all crops that you do not wish to be sprayed.
4. Wash everything thoroughly that has come into contact with the spray.

5. Label all chemicals and keep them out of reach of children.

A further point to remember when spraying is that an insect spray may not always differentiate between the insects you want to get rid of and those that are useful, so don't use your spray indiscriminately.

2

Preparing the soil

So there you are, armed with garden tools, seed packets, stout heart and strong back. Now comes the hard work. The digging. But before you down tools in favour of growing geraniums in a window box, let me assure you that this is the only time you will encounter really hard work in the whole of the gardening year. The secret of good, succulent vegetables is in the preparation of the ground, and that means digging.

Soil comes in many varieties, but for simplicity it can be split into three different categories – light, heavy, and medium. There is no magic formula for finding out which yours is. If you can't tell by looking at it, and quite often you can't, without a very experienced eye, then ask a neighbour, a local seed merchant or nurseryman, or phone the parks and gardens department of your local council.

There are two methods of digging: single spit digging, and double spit digging. If the soil is light, single spit digging may well be enough. If the soil is heavy or medium, then double spit digging is almost essential. A 'spit' incidentally, is the gardening term for a spade's depth, about 30 cm (12 in.). A double spit is therefore twice that, i.e. two spades' depth, or 60 cm (2 ft).

Single spit digging

Make a trench across your plot, the whole width of the plot, one spit deep and 45 cm (18 in.) front to back. Take the

Fork in plant food

Then transfer soil from second trench to first, repeat

earth from this plot and place it along the edge of the bottom end of the plot (see diagram). Fork into the bottom of the trench a 5 cm (2 in.) layer of food for the plants. This food should be manure or Hoof and Horn (alternatively Bonemeal), together with garden peat or, better still, your own garden compost (see Chapter 1).

Double spit digging

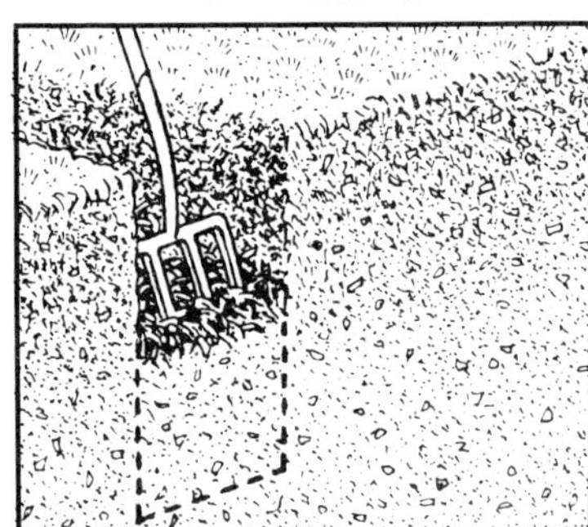

Transfer soil from second trench to first, repeat

Fork in plant food, then dig second spit depth

Place your manure, peat or compost in the bottom of the single spit trench, but this time turn over the earth and feeding agent with a fork to a further depth of 30 cm (12 in.), i.e. another spit. You will need to stand in the trench to do this. All soil benefits from double spit digging, but even heavy soil will need the treatment only once every three or four years.

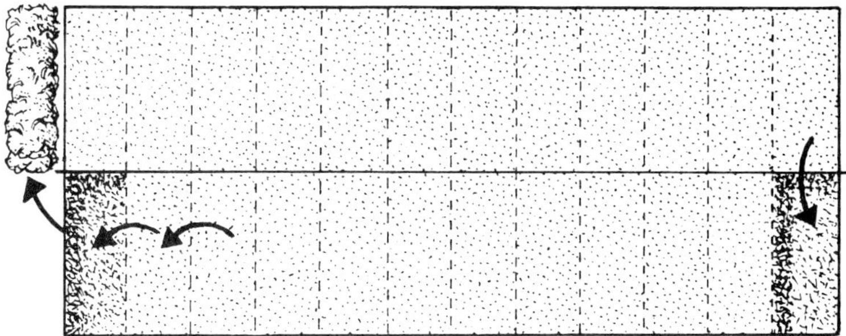

Double spit digging

Once you have forked in your feeding agent, proceed as follows, whether for double or single spit digging. Dig a second trench parallel with the first, filling the first trench with earth from the second. Place your fertilizer in the second trench as before and fill that in with earth from trench three. Proceed in this manner until you reach the end of your plot, where you will find the earth from the first trench waiting to fill the last one.

The above method – taking earth from one end of the plot to the other – requires the use of a wheelbarrow. Do not buy one just for this purpose. Borrow one or else dig your plot in a slightly different way. First, divide the whole plot into two equal parts, lengthwise, so that you have two halves, 7 × 1.5 m (24 × 5 ft). Dig the first trench only to the halfway mark, i.e. to 1.5 m (5 ft) across, and put the earth from this trench on the front edge of the other side of the plot (see diagram, page 24). Continue digging this side of the plot with either double or single spit, whichever is appropriate, placing your manure (or forking it in if using double spit). When you get to the end of the first half of the plot, start digging the second half from the bottom upwards, putting the earth from the first trench on this side into the last trench of the first side. Dig the plot back to the top end where, waiting for you, you will find the earth from the first trench of the first side.

It is unlikely that you found digging and soil preparation to be the most enjoyable of pastimes, but if you survived your double spit dig, you can rest content that the hard labour is over until next year.

Preparing a tilth

Before putting in the seeds there are two important things to do. One is to rake over your soil until it becomes a very fine tilth – the fine top soil in which you will sow your seeds. If you are able to dig the ground over in the autumn, then the winter frost will save you a lot of work by breaking down the soil for you. If, on the other hand, the soil is dug in February, then you will need to put in a lot more work. You will need to hack with the draw hoe to break down the lumps of earth, and you may need to tread with your feet to create the required tilth. Always try to dig over your plot in the autumn, as it will save so much work the following season. Remember, never do a job yourself if nature will do it for you.

Marking the plot

Now for the second important job. Once you have a good tilth, and before you put in your seeds, mark out your sowing layout. In an area as small as our kitchen garden plot, 7 × 3 m (24 × 10 ft), it is vital to plan ahead in order to avoid wasting space. Using your measuring rod, mark out each row paying particular attention to the distance between the rows (see pages 14–15). If the crops are too close they will crowd each other out and fail to develop fully. If they are sown too far apart, you will be wasting precious space, and with a small plot you cannot afford to waste space.

The vegetables placed in our kitchen garden plot are the more popular varieties, but of course you may choose instead any others you prefer – sowing details for both the popular vegetables and the rarer varieties are in the table on pages 27–30. Depending on the amount of space you have, and the appetites of your family, you must decide whether you want to restrict yourself to a plot as small as that of our kitchen garden. Everything that was grown on the original plot is included in the next chapters but you will also find some extras such as onions, aubergines and peppers. If your growing area is restricted, it is sometimes more practical to buy a few young plants rather than occupy valuable space with seed beds. However, in most cases I have also given details on growing from seed.

Sowing and planting guide

Vegetable	*Sowing time*	*Depth of drill*	*Space between rows*	*Transplanting (if applicable)*	*Final space between plants*
Aubergines	March–April	13 mm ($\frac{1}{2}$ in.)*	—	May–June	45 cm (18 in.)
Beans, broad	November–April	10 cm (4 in.)	60 cm (2 ft)	—	10 cm (4 in.)
Beans, Chevrier Vert	April–June	7.5 cm (3 in.)	45 cm (18 in.)	—	10 cm (4 in.)
Beans, dwarf	April–June	7.5 cm (3 in.)	45 cm (18 in.)	—	10 cm (4 in.)
Beans, runner	May–June	10 cm (4 in.) deep 15 cm (6 in.) diameter	120 cm (4 ft)	—	Keep strongest plant per pole or stake
Beets, globe	April–July	4–5 cm ($1\frac{1}{2}$–2 in.)	30 cm (12 in.)	—	5 cm (2 in.)
Broccoli, purple-sprouting	April	2.5 cm (1 in.)	75 cm ($2\frac{1}{2}$ ft)	June	60 cm (2 ft)
Brussels sprouts	March–April	2.5 cm (1 in.)	60–75 cm (2–$2\frac{1}{2}$ ft)	May–*early* June	45 cm (18 in.)
Cabbages, Savoy	April–*early* May	2.5 cm (1 in.)	60 cm (2 ft)	When plants are of planting size	38 cm (15 in.)
Carrots	March–July	2.5–4 cm (1–$1\frac{1}{2}$ in.)	30 cm (12 in.)	—	5 cm (2 in.)
Cauliflowers	May	2.5 cm (1 in.)	60 cm (2 ft)	When plants are of planting size	38 cm (15 in.)
Celeriac	March–April	6 mm ($\frac{1}{4}$ in.)*	—	June	25 cm (10 in.)
Celery, self-blanching	March–April	6 mm ($\frac{1}{4}$ in.)*	Plant in a square block	May–June	23 cm (9 in.) each way

*Best sown in pots or boxes under gentle heat.

Vegetable	*Sowing time*	*Depth of drill*	*Space between rows*	*Transplanting (if applicable)*	*Final space between plants*
Celery, trench	March–April	6 mm ($\frac{1}{4}$ in.)*	120 cm (4 ft)	June–July	Trench: 45 cm (18 in.) deep; 45 cm (18 in.) wide; 30 cm (12 in.) between plants (to take manure or compost). Fill to 30 cm (12 in.) for planting
Courgettes	May–June	4–5 cm ($1\frac{1}{2}$–2 in.) 15 cm (6 in.) dia.	75 cm ($2\frac{1}{2}$ ft) from adjoining crops	—	Single to best plant
Cucumbers	May	4–5 cm ($1\frac{1}{2}$–2 in.) 15 cm (6 in.) dia.	75 cm ($2\frac{1}{2}$ ft) between plants	—	Single to best plant
Garlic	February–March	2.5–4 cm (1–$1\frac{1}{2}$ in.)	38 cm (15 in.)	—	10 cm (4 in.)
Kale	April–May	2.5 cm (1 in.)	60 cm (2 ft)	When plants are of planting size	45 cm (18 in.) between plants
Kohl rabi	April–July	2.5 cm (1 in.)	30 cm (12 in.)	—	7.5 cm (3 in.)
Leeks	April	2.5 cm (1 in.)	45 cm (18 in.)	When 15 cm (6 in.)	15 cm (6 in.) apart
Lettuce	March–July	2.5 cm (1 in.)	30 cm (12 in.)	—	15–30 cm (6–12 in.) depending on variety

Marrows	May–June	4–5 cm ($1\frac{1}{2}$–2 in.) 15 cm (6 in.) dia.	75 cm ($2\frac{1}{2}$ ft) between plants and from adjoining crops	—	Single to best plant
Melons	April	1.3 cm ($\frac{1}{2}$ in.)*	—	June	122 cm (4 ft)
Onions, spring	March–May August–Sept.	2.5–4 cm (1–$1\frac{1}{2}$ in.)	30 cm (12 in.)	—	Thinned by eating
Onions	January (greenhouse) March (outside)	13 mm ($\frac{1}{2}$ in.) in pots under gentle heat 2.5–4 cm (1–$1\frac{1}{2}$ in.) if sown outside	38 cm (15 in.)	From greenhouse in April	7.5–10 cm (3–4 in.)
Parsley	March–July	2.5–4 cm (1–$1\frac{1}{2}$ in.)	30 cm (12 in.)	—	Will thin with use
Parsnips	February–May	2.5–4 cm (1–$1\frac{1}{2}$ in.)	45 cm (18 in.)	—	15–20 cm (6–8 in.)
Peas	March–July	7.5 cm (3 in.) deep 10 cm (4 in.) across	60 cm (2 ft)	—	—
Peas, mange-tout	March–July	7.5 cm (3 in.) deep 10 cm (4 in.) across	90 cm (3 ft)	—	—
Peppers	March–April	13 mm ($\frac{1}{2}$ in.)*	—	May–June	45 cm (18 in.)
Potatoes	March	15–23 cm (6–9 in.)	60 cm (2 ft) (early varieties) 75–90 cm ($2\frac{1}{2}$–3 ft) (late varieties)	—	38 cm (15 in.) (early varieties) 45 cm (18 in.) (late varieties)
Pumpkins	May–June	4–5 cm ($1\frac{1}{2}$–2 in.) 15 cm (6 in.) dia	135 cm ($4\frac{1}{2}$ ft) clearance all round	—	Single to best plant
Radishes, salad	March–September	2.5 cm (1 in.)	25–30 cm (10–12 in.)	—	Thin to single line

* Best sown in pots or boxes under gentle heat.

Vegetable	*Sowing time*	*Depth of drill*	*Space between rows*	*Transplanting (if applicable)*	*Final space between plants*
Radishes, winter	July	2.5 cm (1 in.)	30 cm (12 in.)	—	15 cm (6 in.)
Salsify	April–May	2.5 cm (1 in.)	38 cm (15 in.)	—	20 cm (8 in.)
Scorzonera	April–May	2.5–4 cm (1–1½ in.)	38 cm (15 in.)	—	20 cm (8 in.)
Shallots	February–March	5 cm (2 in.)	30 cm (12 in.)	—	15 cm (6 in.)
Spinach, annual	March–September	2.5 cm (1 in.)	30 cm (12 in.)	—	22 cm (9 in.)
Spinach, perpetual	March–July	5 cm (2 in.)	45 cm (18 in.)	—	15–20 cm (6–8 in.)
Thyme	March–April	4 cm (1½ in.) 15 cm (6 in.) dia.	—	—	—
Tomatoes	—	—	90 cm (3 ft)	Early June	38 cm (15 in.)
Turnips	July	2.5 cm (1 in.)	30 cm (12 in.)	—	10 cm (4 in.)

3

Sowing early seeds

Once the hard work of digging and soil preparation is over, and the plot is marked out in suitable rows, then you can start thinking about sowing the seeds. I give in this and the next two chapters details of how to grow the various vegetables. The order is roughly chronological, starting in this chapter with the earliest sowings and ending with the latest in Chapter 5.

Arm yourself with a good seed catalogue: many of them are free, written by experts and provide an excellent 'read', as well as telling all you need to know of the characteristics of the various seeds you want to plant. Choose vegetables which will prosper in your type of soil.

Usually there will be far more seeds in the packet than are required for the initial sowing. Heavy sowing will result in weak seedlings and great difficulty in thinning out. Even if you are lucky, with plenty of sowing space, little and often is the rule, to keep a good succession of young, fresh crops and to avoid having far more than you can use at any one period.

Having read your catalogue, send for the seeds early. Don't delay sending off for them until the day before you need to sow them. When the seeds arrive, read the back of the seed packet carefully – you will find there sowing instructions that have been written by experts. Always allow for slight variations in the sowing depth. For instance, light soils will probably need slightly deeper sowings.

As the season progresses into May and June, many of the seedlings will need to be thinned and singled. Some, like cabbages, will need to be transplanted to their final growing place. Around this time you should also purchase tomatoes for planting out.

Fortunately, not everything in the garden will need thinning out. Parsley and spring onions will probably have been thinned out as you picked them for the table. There are three golden rules for thinning and singling. First, choose a cool cloudy day – and that shouldn't be too difficult in England. A recent shower of rain can be a great advantage, because it goes a long way towards helping the seedling left in the ground to recover. Secondly, do not try to hurry the job. Take time and do it carefully, remembering that those plants left in the ground will be providing the kitchen with vegetables for the rest of the year. The third rule is to finish the job with gentle hoeing. And one more rule – don't forget to put the thinned-out rejected vegetables on the compost heap!

January sowings

There is little anyone can achieve outside in this month but, although the normal onion crop will not be sown until March, if you've a mind to have a crack at your local show, now is the time to begin – provided you are lucky enough to have a small greenhouse. Should you not be fortunate to own a greenhouse, much can still be achieved on a table beside a south facing window.

Onions

In the first week of the month onion seed should be sown thinly in pots or trays in a gentle heat of not less than 7°C (45°F).

As soon as the seedlings are big enough to handle, transplant them into another tray, this time about 7.5 cm (3 in.) apart, then finally transplant to the permanent outdoor position in about April. It is impossible to lay down rules about the ideal time for this final move to an unprotected outdoor climate. It will depend on the prevailing weather conditions and the part of the country you live in. With your heart full of optimism, you will plant them 23 cm (9 in.) apart, leaving plenty of room for championship growth! Once the foliage is well advanced you can start feeding.

A few hints

Here are a couple of warnings about growing onions, whether you want them for a table or are hoping for prize contenders.

First, in a damp and dull season all onions are subject to mildew. They will take on a slightly grey, powdery look and the tips will wither. As soon as you notice this, spray or dust them with sulphur, repeating the process after ten or fourteen days if necessary. This should check the mildew.

Secondly, when you're harvesting onions, never pull them out of the ground. Always lift them with a fork. That way you'll minimize the risk of damaging them, which can reduce their storage life.

Finally, here's a tip if you're really keen on your onions and would like an extra-early crop. Buy yourself a packet of a relatively new seed that can be sown in August. It's a variety of a Japanese hybrid and is called Kaizuka Extra Early. It can be sown in the open in August and thinned down to 7.5 cm (3 in.) as soon as the seedlings are big enough. They should live quite happily through the winter and you will be lifting them up to six weeks earlier than a normal crop.

Another January 'greenhouse' tip is to sow a few cabbage seeds in a pot, which, after potting on into single pots, will be ready to plant out in April. Hispi and June Star are suitable varieties to mature in May to June.

February sowings

The second of your seeds to go into the plot are broad beans. This is one of the earliest of the new season's crops, and in the early summer when they are young and at their best they make a welcome change from the winter greens of the earlier months. There can be nothing better than fresh broad beans and parsley sauce from your own garden in late May.

Broad beans

Pot planting

February can be unpredictable, with glorious spring sunshine one year, and below zero frosts the next. As a general rule it is usually safe to sow beans out of doors in February in the south of England, unless the weather happens to be singularly inclement, but what happens if you live in the north? What if the weather is wet and cold? Do not despair! Broad beans, and many other crops, can be started in pots or boxes inside the garden shed, or some other frost-free place. Choose a 10 cm (4 in.) pot, and place in it either a proprietary brand of potting compost, or a mixture of your own soil and peat, firm the soil down and push the bean well in. Fill the pot, leaving room for watering. Beans in pots should be well watered initially and kept in a dark, frost-free shed.

Beans can also be grown in boxes. Place some stones or broken pieces of pot in the bottom of the box to assist in the drainage, and plant the beans about 5 cm (2 in.) apart.

Whether they have been started in pots or boxes, keep the beans in the dark shed until their shoots start breaking through the surface of the soil, then transfer them to a much lighter place. Later when they are about 7.5–10 cm (3–4 in.) high they will be ready to plant out, and with any luck the weather will have improved by then and will no longer be a threat to young seedlings. It is a good idea when planting out your seedlings to plant some seeds straight into the ground at the same time. These seeds will mature later thereby providing a succession of broad beans.

Sowing

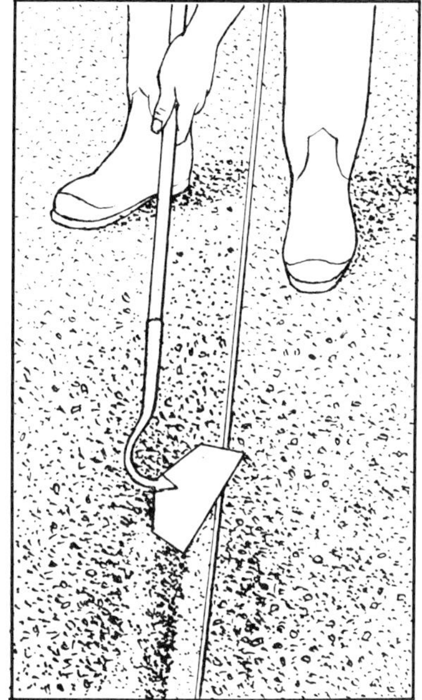
Making a V-shaped drill

If you are lucky enough to live in a fairly mild part of the country, you can sow your broad bean seeds straight into the ground. They are rather large and therefore need to be sown quite deeply. For a single row, you will need to make a V-shaped drill about 10 cm (4 in.) deep. Mark out the drill, using a line for guidance. This will keep the row neat and straight and will also help to avoid wasting useful space. Take the draw hoe and 'draw' it through the soil a few times, parallel to the line. In drawing the drill try not to put too much of the displaced earth at one end or the other. It should be evenly distributed. The beans should be planted when you have achieved a depth of about 10 cm (4 in.) with the draw hoe. Place the beans about 5 cm (2 in.) apart along the drill. This may seem too close for comfort, but you will be thinning them out later to about 10 cm (4 in.) apart.

This is not as wasteful as it may seem. You will still have more seeds left in the packet than you can possibly use, and by planting twice as many as you actually need, you will give yourself a useful insurance policy against the hazards of nature and predators such as birds and mice and slugs. They get hungry too, and will enjoy a good meal from your seeds. Incidentally, it matters not a jot which way the beans go into the drill. Whether they are put in flat or sideways or on end, nature has her own way of coping with human cack-handedness, and no matter which way you have put them in, the shoots will come up and the roots will go down! In a good year outdoor sowings will not be far behind those started in pots.

Of course, the plot should have been carefully marked out beforehand to avoid wasting space, but if you haven't already marked out the broad bean row, then mark it before you fill in the drill, otherwise when you return to your plot, maybe in two or three days' time, you will have to guess where you planted your beans and your guesswork could be out by 30cm (12 in.) either way. As a result you may either waste space, or worse still, dig up the beans you have just planted! Once you have marked the drill it is safe to fill it. Push the earth into the drill with the hoe, covering the beans, and finally give the ground a light raking over to prevent any hard pans forming.

Thinning

When the plants are big enough to handle – 7.5–10cm (3–4 in.) – it is time to start thinning them out to 10cm (4 in.) apart. In effect, this means removing every other plant. Pull out the thinnings by hand, protecting the two neighbouring plants as you do so by using the edges of your hand to hold the soil firm against the plants that are to remain. Of course, if you started your beans in the garden shed you can avoid this stage by planting them out 10cm (4 in.) apart in the first place.

Transplanting

Broad beans are perfectly amenable to transplanting, so if there are gaps in your rows as a result of non-germination or for any other reason, you can transplant some of your thinnings to fill those gaps. *But* don't pull out any young plant that you aim to transplant; lift it carefully with a trowel so that the root is not damaged. Make sure you leave a good big ball of soil round the root, having previously prepared a hole with your trowel big enough to take the root with the soil round it.

Of course, you may have been lucky and there are no gaps through non-germination. But if you have some space available in your garden you can still lift all your thinnings with a trowel and transplant them, creating new rows of broad beans. The transplanted ones will naturally suffer a check, which means that they will produce their crop somewhat later than those that have not been disturbed. This is no great hardship, however, as it means that your crop will be spread over a longer period.

Hoeing and feeding

Regular hoeing along the sides of the rows will be much appreciated by the plants. A light feeding with general fertilizer, again all along the sides of the rows, and well hoed in, will also promote growth. This is especially advisable if you haven't the time or opportunity to manure the ground before sowing the seed.

Spraying

One little problem that Mother Nature is likely to land in your lap is blackfly. There are two ways of coping with this.

First, when the plant is in full flower, remove the tip of the growing stem – the one right in the centre of the top showing a flush of vigorous foliage.

The other way is to spray with insecticide before the plant comes into flower. (If you adopt this method remember to spray not only above but underneath the leaves as well.) There is a special reason for doing this before the plant comes into flower. The insecticide you use is a systemic chemical spray that permeates the foliage, and the insects and pests then feed on it.

If you spray the plant when it is in full flower, remember that the victims are likely to include the bumblebees that can be so useful to other parts of the garden.

Varieties

Aquadulce Claudia is a suitable early variety and a couple of other varieties likely to give you a good season of broad beans are Giant Windsor and Unrivalled Green Windsor. But if you are really after show-size beans try Colossal – the name really means what it says!

French beans

For dwarf French beans I suggest a variety called Chevrier Vert, because it is very versatile and can be used in three stages of growth. First as *haricots verts*, when they are in the fresh green state (top and tail them and boil them as they are). Second as *haricots flageolets* (shell and eat as tender green beans), and finally as *haricots secs*, in other words dry white beans (particularly useful as they store easily and can be used in the winter). Another excellent regular variety is the Sprite, a tender stringless type.

Here's a hint for parents if the kids pretend not to like these white beans. Just tell them that they're not much different from the beans that are turned into baked beans in tomato sauce.

For cultivation follow the advice given for broad beans, but the initial drill need not be more than 7.5 cm (3 in.) deep.

4

Moving into spring

March sowings

There are a number of crops to be sown in March. Generally speaking, potatoes, carrots, parsnips, parsley, peas, spring onions, radishes and spinach go into the plot at this time of year together with sprout seed to produce plants for transplanting to permanent positions in early or mid-May. Aubergines, peppers and tomatoes should be sown in the greenhouse in pots in March if gentle heating is available, prior to planting out in May or June. It is difficult to be specific about planting times as they will vary according to weather conditions and also to the part of the country in which you are living. Dates given for planting either in this book or on the back of a seed packet should be regarded merely as a guideline, not as holy writ.

Potatoes

The dear old spud might well be called king of root crops. An uncrowned king at one time maybe, but now surely a king with a crown of gold, if some fairly recent shop prices are anything to go by. So although our original kitchen garden plot only catered for a few earlies, you will probably now be interested in a good-sized crop.

Sowing

To set about growing a sizeable quantity of potatoes, either earlies or main crop, first dig or draw a drill 15–23 cm

(6–9 in.) deep. The width of your spade will decide the width of the drill. On the flat bottom of the drill spread a 5 cm (2 in.) layer of moist peat. This is not essential but if you take this extra bit of trouble you will probably harvest a better crop of potatoes.

For earlies, the tubers need to be 38 cm (15 in.) apart and if you're planting more than one row then leave 60 cm (2 ft) between the rows. For the main crop leave a gap of about 45 cm (18 in.) between the tubers and the rows need to be 75 cm to 90 cm (2 ft 6 in. to 3 ft) apart. To cover in the drill, bring the soil in from the sides using a hoe.

Earthing up

When the potatoes are showing about 15–23 cm (6–9 in.) of foliage the time has come for what is known as earthing

'Earthing up' of the potatoes is done when the tops are 15 cm (6 in.) to 23 cm (9 in.). Apply a light dressing of general fertilizer along both sides of the row before earthing up.

up. Take a draw hoe and pull the earth up vigorously to the foliage on both sides of the row. The main reason for doing this is to keep the actual potatoes well covered with soil as they grow, so that the ones near the surface don't turn green. A secondary reason is that it will make it easier for you to weed between the rows. To assist the growth of the crop, try sprinkling a light dressing of general fertilizer along both sides of the row before earthing up.

Staking

Potatoes are not normally staked, but if you are sticking to the limited space on our kitchen garden plot, it may prove necessary. Potato greenery is liable to spread itself and fall over nearby crops, causing the neighbouring plants to fight their way through the potato leaves and in doing so, to become leggy. Four short canes about 120cm (4ft) long should be placed one at each corner of the potato plot. Tie raffia round the perimeter of the potato plot from cane to cane. As the potato top growth increases, tie another line about the first, and put in more canes if necessary.

Earlies

If your taste buds react in any way like my own you will have a special fancy for those first small earlies with their outstanding flavour. So here's an idea for treating yourself to some extra earlies

In mid-February buy some 23cm (9in.) black polythene containers and fill each one with John Innes No. 1 compost. Put in one potato tuber and keep it indoors, under the stairs or, if you have a greenhouse, under the bench. Then as soon as you see the shoots coming through, move the container to a really light but frost-free place – still indoors, of course, but really light, and preferably cool. If there is too much warmth the plant will be forced, resulting in a magnificent top but with no potatoes underneath. Let them finish the rest of their growth indoors and you will have a good chance of impressing your family with mouth-watering new potatoes by the end of May.

A spud for Christmas

Another out-of-the-ordinary idea is to grow some new potatoes to be dug on Christmas morning to accompany the roast turkey. Plant two or three tubers out in the open garden in late August and with a bit of luck you will have the results ready for Christmas Day. I am afraid that this ploy cannot be guaranteed successful – so much depends on the weather and the state of the ground – but since three or four tubers take up so little space you really have nothing to lose by having a go.

Carrots and parsnips

First, a word of warning about carrots and parsnips, for they are subject to a little problem called 'forking'. What happens is that one individual root comes up with twin stems, frequently knobbly and misshapen. Although it is still edible in this form it is not merely unattractive but a lot more is wasted. The cause of this mishap is quite simple – fresh manure. The solution is equally simple – avoid planting carrots and parsnips in freshly manured ground.

Sowing

Start by making a drill with the draw hoe. The seed for carrots and parsnips must always go in rather thinly. It's worth taking trouble over this, because it will save you a lot of bother later when it comes to thinning out. In the case of carrots a light sprinkling of calomel 4 per cent dust along the drill for the seeds is advisable, for it will help to eliminate the possibility of carrot root fly later on.

Thinning

Carrots must be thinned to 5 cm (2 in.) apart and parsnips, as they grow rather larger, to 10 cm (4 in.) apart. Alternatively, you can do a first thinning of the parsnips to 5 cm (2 in.) apart and then a second thinning, taking out alternate young parsnips. You can use these for the table, leaving the rest to grow on to full size.

Growing prize specimens

A lot of fun and satisfaction can be had from growing a prize specimen for the local horticultural show and it is perfectly possible to have a go at this even if you are a novice gardener. I am told that a parsnip weighing as much as 4.5 kg (10 lb) has been grown! But you don't need to be that ambitious to produce a very reasonable specimen for showing.

Sowing. Your first requirement for growing a prize parsnip is, amazingly enough, a crowbar or similar tool. Stab this vigorously into the ground, making a circular motion at the same time, so that you end up with a funnel-shaped hole about 75 cm (2 ft 6 in.) deep. If you want to grow prize carrots, the funnel will be only 45 cm (18 in.) deep. The last part of this stabbing operation is best done with a thin cane so that the funnel tapers off to a very fine point. It is best not to attempt to prepare your funnel when the ground is very

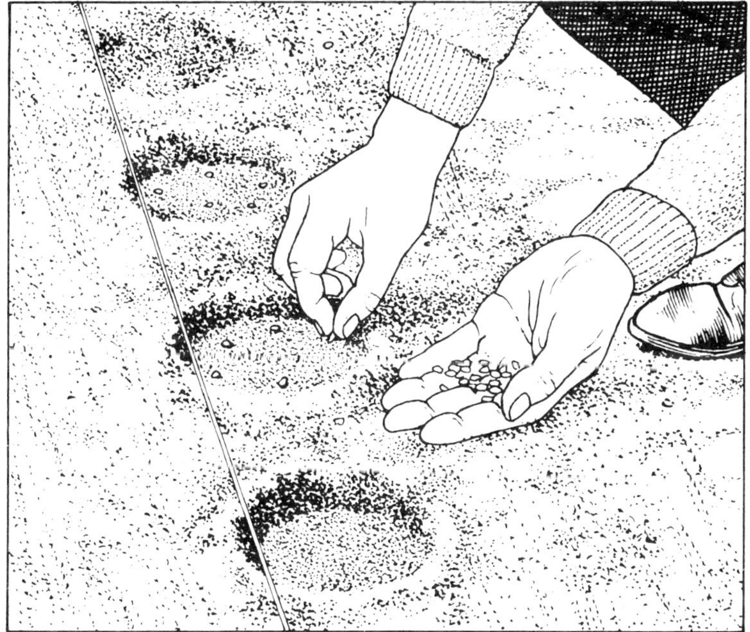

Sowing seeds for championship-size parsnips or carrots at the top of the carefully-filled 'funnel'. It's worth taking some time to prepare the funnels.

dry and dusty, because the whole point of the circular movement of the crowbar is to make the sides of the funnel very firm, and moist soil will make the job simpler.

Now fill the funnel with a good loam or John Innes No. 1 compost. It is vital that this filling should be well tamped down. To be sure of this, do the filling in three or four stages, and use the cane again for tamping the loam at the bottom of the funnel. Obviously, as you get nearer the top of the funnel the tamping will need to be done with a wider and more substantial instrument. When you have reached about 6 mm ($\frac{1}{4}$ in.) from the top of the funnel place four or five seeds, well spaced out, on the loam and then cover them over with more loam until it is level with the soil.

To give you some idea of the care and thoroughness needed for this task, you can reckon on taking fifteen to twenty minutes for the whole operation. Do not be tempted to transplant your best seedling to the centre of the funnel, that way will only guarantee failure.

Thinning. When the seedlings are large enough to handle, thin them down to just one, preferably the one nearest the middle (assuming nature has obliged and turned out a good-looking specimen in that desirable position). This method of parsnip and carrot cultivation is also of use where your garden soil will not produce good crops sown in drills.

Feeding. And now for feeding. This is where your firm-sided funnel is very useful, because it takes the feed where you want it. Don't give in to the temptation to overfeed. A light liquid feed about every ten to fourteen days once the vegetable is well formed will be adequate. Overfeeding or over-rich soil may cause canker, and that certainly won't give you a prize specimen!

Have a go at it. It won't take up much space and if you don't fancy entering the local horticultural show you can always get four or five of your neighbours to join a friendly competition to see who can grow the largest parsnip. It should provide a good meal, too, by the time it is fully grown. (Mind you, to be honest, I personally prefer young, tiny and succulent vegetables every time.)

Peas

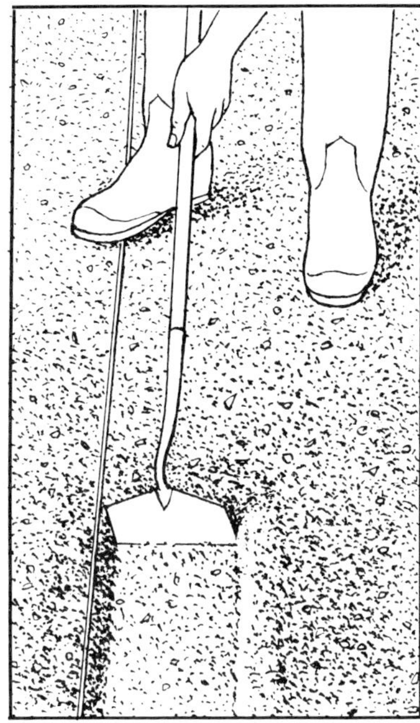

Making a flat-bottomed drill

Peas are another large seed, and they are sown in a flat-bottomed drill. On our kitchen garden plot this was a full 3 m (10 ft) long row, the full width of the plot. Again it is advisable to mark this out with a line to help keep the row straight.

Sowing

Draw a drill some 10 cm (4 in.) wide and 7.5–10 cm (3–4 in.) deep, then scatter the seed along the bottom of the drill so that they end up about 4 cm ($1\frac{1}{2}$ in.) apart. Err on the side of generosity – you can always lose a few in the course of growing but you can't possibly catch up later.

Feeding and spraying

Feeding should not be necessary unless you have decided to grow for exhibition purposes, but it is a good idea to spray with a systemic insecticide when the plants are about 5–7.5 cm (2–3 in.) high. This pre-emptive attack is aimed at discouraging a little beastie called the pea weevil.

Staking

Peas benefit from a limited amount of staking. Use twiggy sticks, about 90 cm (3 ft) high, and remember to put them in the ground before sowing the peas. Staking peas keeps them from trailing on the ground, thus preventing mould. It also helps them to ripen by holding them upwards to the sun. If twiggy sticks are difficult to come by, canes placed along the row at intervals – with strings run right round the crop – will prove a good substitute.

Varieties

A good early variety that has several advantages is Kelvedon Wonder. It is mildew-resistant and is therefore very useful in a damp season. It is also handy for catch cropping (see Chapter 5), as well as requiring an absolute minimum of twig support.

Earlies

However skilful the frozen-food merchants become, there is no way they can match the superb flavour of freshly picked peas. And by carefully selecting varieties you can grow your own peas right through the season. For a particularly early crop some varieties, such as Meteor, can be sown in November. They will live quite happily through the winter and you should have peas on your table in the month of May. Admittedly, they may not be quite as tasty as the spring sowing, but I reckon anything that comes out of the garden early tastes good anyway. One other way of getting an early crop is to sow the peas in pots and then bed them out as soon as the weather becomes favourable.

Growing prize peas

As always, growing for showing calls for rather more time and attention. Show Perfection is the variety to remember, as it will grow to a height of 1.2–1.5 m (4–5 ft).

Sowing. The starting-point, as always, is thorough preparation of the soil. This means double spit digging and stacks of humus. (This also applies to sweet peas if you have a mind to brighten up your vegetable plot with some gaily coloured flowers.) Once the ground is ready, in go the canes. Place them 30 cm (12 in.) apart, because you will be growing one individual plant to a cane. Sow four seeds round each cane, then single down to the best-looking plant when they are about 13 cm (5 in.) high. As an alternative, you can start off the plants in pots.

Care and attention. From here on you are going to have to control the growth of each plant and this includes cutting off the tendrils as they appear. These are the long wispy tentacles that wrap themselves round the cane. So you will need to provide alternative support by tying where necessary with raffia. Also, remove the side shoots lower down – you want to end up with just the right amount of growth to concentrate the power of the plant where you need it. The plant must flower exactly twenty-one days before the date of the show, so as to produce just the right kind of pod for showing, and, with luck, prize-winning.

An application of Sevin dust will help to prevent maggot. There is also one all-important point that came as a surprise to me when I first heard about it, and that is that you should never touch the pods with your fingers. If you do, you will leave very distinctive finger marks on them, thus spoiling the 'bloom'. Try it on a couple of pods and you'll soon see what I mean. The trick is to hold the pod by the stalk only from the time you pick it to the time it goes on show.

That is just a brief outline of how to set about growing peas for showing. If you are really fired with enthusiasm for exhibition work it is time to turn to a book by an expert, or to consult your local horticultural society.

Sowing smaller seeds

Smaller seeds do not need to be sown so deeply. Generally speaking, the smaller the seed the shallower the drill, but as regards drill size and other sowing suggestions, always be guided by the instructions on the back of the seed packets and also allow for the nature of your soil. Many of the kitchen garden seeds are of the smaller variety. Brussels sprouts, cabbage, kale, carrots, lettuce, radish, spring onion and parsley are all sown in a similar way.

Parsley

Let's take parsley as an example. Here are sowing details for that seed. Draw a drill 2.5–4 cm (1–1½ in.) deep. Pour some of the seeds from the packet into one palm, and then with the thumb and forefinger of the other hand, distribute the seeds gently and evenly along the drill. Parsley can be sown fairly thickly, as it will get frequent thinning through use.

The method used to fill the shallow drill is entirely different from that used to fill the deeper type. This time you will need to 'edge' the earth into the drill with your feet, using a method that looks part way between a military two-step and a dance some readers may remember called the Creep. The idea behind this curious soft-shoe shuffle is to return the soil to the drill without disturbing the tiny seeds you have just put in, and to firm the earth down to exclude any air pockets, without making the ground as hard as cement in the process. Stand with your feet apart on either side of the row and slowly shuffle and twist your toes in and out, edging the soil back into the drill as you do so. Stop every metre (every yard or so) and gently tap down on top of the drill with one foot while keeping the weight of the body on the other. Make it a very gentle operation; remember the seeds in that drill are very, very small. When the drill is finished and firmed down, give it a finish with a light raking over.

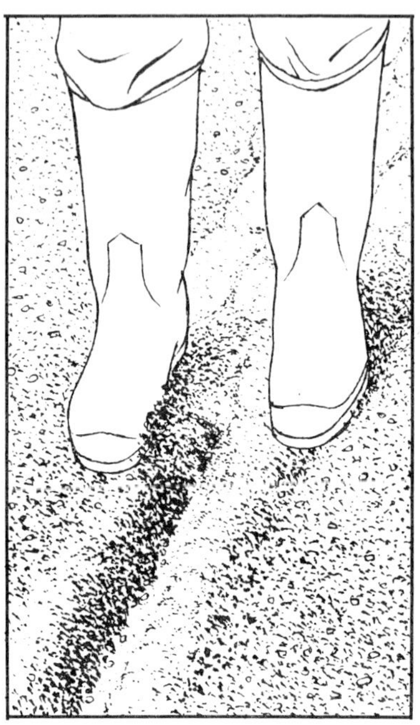

Returning the soil to the drill

Radishes, lettuces and spring onions

Other small seeds for March sowing are treated similarly. Radishes and lettuces should be sown less thickly, since you will need to thin them out later in the growing season. On the other hand, you should not need to thin out your spring onions which are thinned automatically as you pick out the young ones to eat. When planting spring onion it is advisable to sprinkle the drill very lightly with calomel 4 per cent dust, to take care of the root fly.

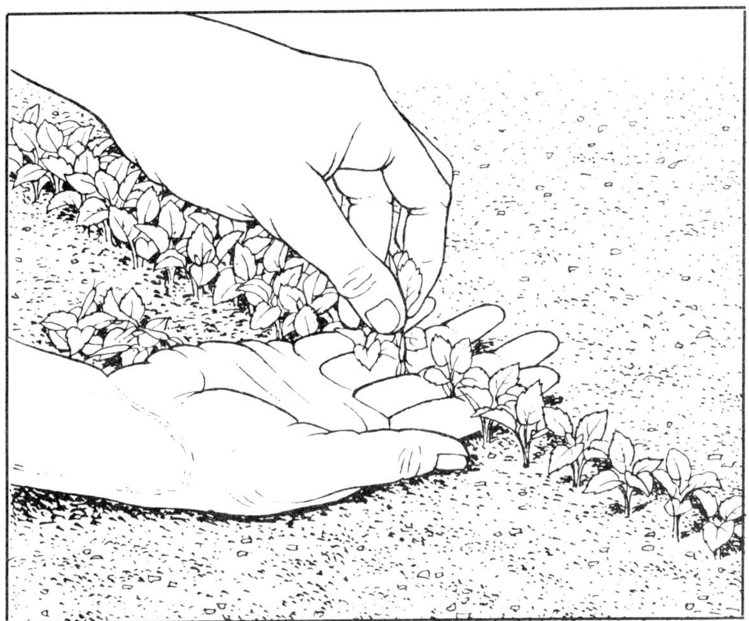

Thinning radishes

To thin radishes and indeed all small plants, place the hand upside-down underneath the plant with the back of the hand on the ground to keep the hand steady, then gently tease out the unwanted seedlings with the fingers.

Thin out the radishes to a single row, taking care not to disturb those that remain. Some of them may fall over or look rather sad. There is nothing to worry about, they should perk up within twenty-four hours. When you have thinned out sufficiently, give the ground a careful hoeing with a dutch hoe, hoeing the soil on either side of the row. This is like tucking a baby back in bed – you've disturbed the blankets and your plants need the warmth and security of the bedclothes, so tuck them up again. It is all a very gentle process, filling the air pockets and helping the seedlings that remain to stand up for themselves again.

Lettuces are singled rather than thinned. Eventually they will need to be 15–23 cm (6–9 in.) apart, but for the time being thin them to a 5 cm (2 in.) spacing first as a protection against failure. Then, in about two weeks, you will be able to thin them yet again to a final 15–23 cm (6–9 in.) apart at the second thinning.

Brussels sprouts

One way of making sure that you have fresh vegetables from your garden right through the year (or almost) is to grow lots of lovely brassicas – the posh name for greens. This is also the most important crop of vegetables from the point of view of your health, providing an excellent source of vitamin C during the winter.

Sowing

Start by preparing a seed bed. An area 2.5 cm (8 ft) long by 60 cm (2 ft) wide will be large enough to give you eight rows each 60 cm (2 ft) long with 30 cm (12 in.) between the rows. If you think that a row 60 cm (2 ft) long is rather limited I promise you that it can produce more than enough seedling for your own use. If you try growing more you will be well on the way to becoming a market gardener.

Prepare a drill about 2.5 cm (1 in.) deep, but before putting the seeds in remember the problem of club root and give the drill a quick sprinkling of calomel 4 per cent dust. By the way, this applies to all brassica sowings, as they are all at risk from club root. To keep one step ahead of nature, namely the flea beetle, an application of Sevin dust as the seedlings break through the soil is also advisable.

Transplanting

Transplant the seedlings when they are about 15 cm (6 in.) tall, lifting them with a fork. Select the most healthy and vigorous-looking plants and throw away anything that looks spindly or has a woody stem. There are now three different ways of bedding the plants.

Method 1. This is the basic system. Use a dibber to make a generous hole so that the roots will not be curled up or cramped. The depth should be the same as the depth of the seedling when you lifted it from the ground. The vital point at this stage is to ensure that the roots of the plant are thoroughly firmed in. Pressing the soil down at the top when the hole is completely filled is just not enough – make sure that the soil is properly firmed round the roots before you fill the hole. There is a simple test to make sure that the seedling is properly bedded: place the back of your hand on the ground with two fingers round the stem of the plant and pull gently. If the plant moves at all it is not bedded firmly enough. There is no need to water if the ground is moist.

Method 2. If you are putting in only a few plants use a trowel to make the holes. If the ground is particularly dry each hole can be filled with water, which should be allowed to soak away before you put in the plant. Firm in as above.

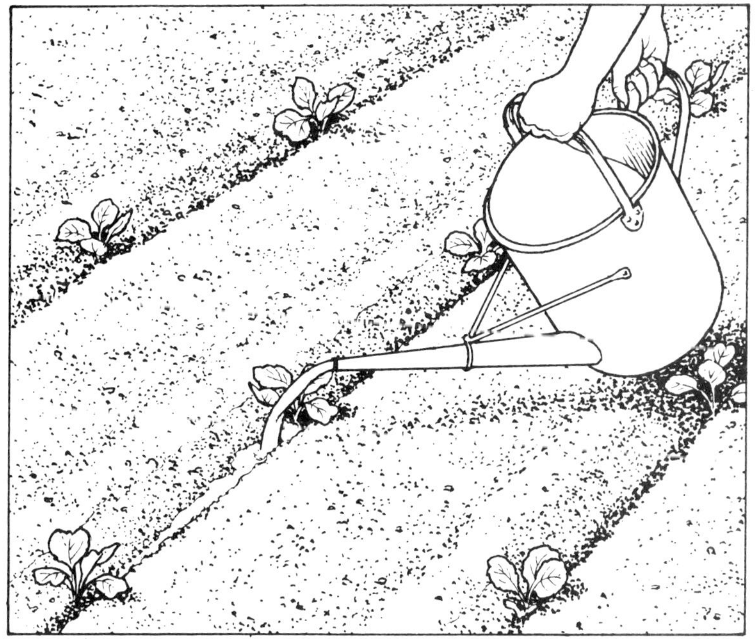

One way of combating the prospect of very dry weather. The 7.5 cm (3 in.) drill helps contain the moisture

Method 3. Using a draw hoe, draw a V-shaped drill about 7.5 cm (3 in.) deep. Then use a dibber to make the holes and complete the planting as in Method 1. Now water the length of the drill. This method is particularly advantageous in very dry weather, as it contains the moisture where it is most needed as well as giving the plants a little extra protection.

Extra hints

Brussels sprouts can be spaced 75 cm (2 ft 6 in.) apart in each direction, or alternatively 60 cm (2 ft) apart with 90 cm (3 ft) between the rows. They like a lot of space because they are very hungry plants. However, if your plot is very small and these figures make you wonder if you will have room for anything else, then 60 × 60 cm (2 × 2 ft) should provide quite reasonable results.

Recommended varieties

If you are madly keen on sprouts and want them on your plate as early as possible, early varieties like Early Half Fall or Peer Gynt can be considered. Later varieties include Market Rearguard and Citadel.

Aubergines and peppers

Aubergines and peppers are associated in many people's minds with the balmy climate of Mediterranean areas, but in fact they have been grown successfully in southern England for a year or two now, even out in the open.

Sowing

Sowing is the same for both plants. Put seven seeds, suitably spaced, into a 10 cm (4 in.) pot filled with John Innes No. 1 compost. Cover the seeds with a spot more John Innes and then water, using a fine rose. Keep at a minimum temperature of 13°C (55°F).

Potting on

The next stage is potting on. When the plants are big enough to handle, transfer each seedling to its own individual 10 cm (4 in.) pot. If you are particularly keen to succeed with these plants a further potting on to 15 cm (6 in.) pots is worthwhile, but this is not essential.

Planting out

If you have sown the seeds in March the plants should be ready to go out in the garden at the end of May or the beginning of June, after a few days of hardening off.

Picking out the ends of the side shoots is necessary for peppers once a fair number of fruits is set, to concentrate the strength of the plant into the fruit. Pinch out the top of the aubergine plant when it is 15–23 cm (6–9 in.) high to encourage side growths, because these are the ones that will bear fruit. The number of fruits should be limited to six or even as few as four or they will be too small to be of any use to you.

Feeding and protection

Both peppers and aubergines need regular feeding. Although both can be grown in the open in a sunny, sheltered spot there is no doubt that protection by cloches will make a big difference, especially in the early stages.

Tomatoes

Although the tomato is usually categorized as a fruit, I shall deal with it here in the vegetable section because the methods employed to grow tomatoes have more in common with vegetable growing than with fruit growing.

Of all the crops that may be attempted by the kitchen gardener the one that is likely to give you most satisfaction and enjoyment at your first attempt is tomatoes. They can be grown in open ground, or in the soil of the greenhouse floor, or under glass by the ring culture method, or in pots or boxes on a balcony or patio, or even in a window box. Most gardeners who want six to a dozen plants are likely to buy their plants (from a nurseryman or garden shop) ready grown to a height of about 15–20 cm (6–8 in.) ready for transplanting into outdoor or greenhouse soil. The method is the same either way, though of course the dates will vary.

But why not enjoy the fun of growing your tomatoes from seed? Admittedly, you may well end up with far more plants than you need, but then you have the opportunity of selecting the strongest plants and throwing away the rest – and you may well have enough left over to make gifts to your gardening friends.

Timing

If you are going to grow your tomatoes under glass for the whole of their life you can start sowing seeds as early as December. Then your 15 cm (6 in.) plants will go into the greenhouse soil some time in March if you can maintain a temperature of 16°C (60°F), or at least a month later if your greenhouse doesn't have artificial heating. If your plants are going to be out in the open, sow the seeds under cover in March or April for planting out in early June. Needless to say, with the vagaries of the British climate you must keep your fingers crossed that there won't be a nasty late frost. If your greenhouse can only accommodate a few plants, tomatoes can be germinated in the airing cupboard and potted to grow in a light, warm windowsill.

Sowing

Fill a seed tray to within 13 mm ($\frac{1}{2}$ in.) of the top with John Innes No. 1 compost. Sow the seeds lightly and evenly over the surface and then cover with a thin sprinkling of the same compost. Tap down very lightly, and finally damp over with a fine-rosed watering can. For this initial stage of growth cover the seed tray with a sheet of glass and on top of that place a sheet of newspaper – both these must be removed as soon as the seedlings start to show through. A minimum temperature of 16°C (60°F) is essential, but your embryo crop will like you even more if you can keep them at something like 18–21°C (65–70°F). If you really think it is a waste to sow a whole seed tray, sow a small number of seeds in something like a 15 cm (6 in.) pot, using the same methods as already described.

Transplanting

As soon as the seedlings are big enough to handle, they are ready for transplanting into individual 7.5 cm (3 in.) pots. But, you may ask, just how big is big enough to handle? The answer to that one is the same as to 'how long is a piece of string?' The real experts like to tackle this operation at the earliest possible moment, with a view to disturbing the roots as little as possible. The longer they stay in the seed tray the bigger and more bushy the roots become, so the disturbance is bound to be greater. So, if you feel confident enough, transplant when the seedlings are about 19 mm ($\frac{3}{4}$ in.) high. But if your fingers are all thumbs nothing terrible will happen if you wait a bit longer.

Ease each seedling out of the soil with a small and delicate instrument (one of those pointed wooden plant labels will do perfectly), taking great care not to damage the root and holding the seedling only by one of the two leaves that have done the job of breaking through the soil. Never hold the seedling by the stem.

Before lifting the seedlings you will have prepared whatever number of pots you have decided on. Choose 7.5–9 cm (3–3$\frac{1}{2}$ in.) pots. Clay, plastic or black polythene will do equally well. Even empty, cleaned-out yoghurt pots can be pressed into service if you have had the forethought to save enough, but don't forget to punch one or two holes in the bottom for drainage. For the same reason, all kinds of pots need a few small stones or pebbles in the bottom before you fill them with John Innes No. 1 compost. This needs to be tamped down, leaving 6 mm ($\frac{1}{4}$ in.) between the top of the compost and the rim of the pot. Now make a generous hole in the centre of the compost with a pencil or any similar mini-dibber – the vital thing here is that the hole should be big enough to avoid compressing the root in any way. Lower the seedling into the hole and lightly firm in.

Your seedlings will grow on in this environment until they are at least 15 cm (6 in.) tall and ready for transplanting.

Patio and balcony plants

If you plan to grow a few fine tomatoes on your patio or balcony then you will pot on. This means transplanting the 15 cm (6 in.) plant from the 7.5 cm (3 in.) pot to something like a 25 cm (10 in.) pot. Here you have a choice of using straightforward garden soil, John Innes No. 2 compost or ordinary soil with some John Innes and/or peat mixed with it. The pot for the patio can again be clay, plastic or black polythene, or the composition type known as whalehide. Watering is a straightforward matter: just remember that rather than 'little and often', your plants will need a thorough watering at well-spaced intervals. This will obviously depend on the weather, but intervals of from ten days to three weeks will be about right.

Staking

One important thing to remember is that as the plants grow they will need supporting by a stake. It is essential to get this stake in the ground before transplanting. If you don't keep to this sequence and put the plant in the ground first, followed by the stake, the stake may well go through the root of the plant, causing irreparable damage. So remember, always stake first. This applies equally if you are growing your tomatoes on the patio in 25 cm (10 in.) pots.

Another method of supporting the growing plant is to dangle a long piece of string from a taut wire some 1.8 m (6 ft) above the ground, stretched between two rigid posts, and attach the plant to the string. This system is more suitable for greenhouse cultivation, whereas stakes are easier to handle out-of-doors.

Planting out

Now you are ready to transplant the tomato plant from the pot into the ground. Make sure that the hole you dig with a trowel is big enough by slipping in an empty pot of the appropriate size before attempting to transplant. The space between tomato plants should be 45 cm (1 ft 6 in.) each way.

Tying

Now we come to tying the plants. This needs to be done for all plants, whether they are grown indoors or out-of-doors, in pots or in ring culture – I'll be coming to that in a minute.

Always remember to put the stake in before the plant in order not to damage the roots. Except for the bush type, all tomatoes need plenty of support. For a greenhouse crop, string hanging from a taut wire may be used instead of stakes

Warning: *Always tie below a leaf joint and never below a truss*

As the tomato plant steadily grows taller make sure that it always has adequate support by tying it at intervals to the stake. The string or raffia must be passed under a leaf joint and never, repeat never, under the truss. The first tie will be under the leaf joint immediately below the first truss. Take the string or raffia once round the plant – not too tightly because the stem will thicken and draw the string tight of its own accord – and then twice round the stake to prevent slipping.

Setting the fruit

Setting the fruit is what you do as each truss appears. You need to give it a light spray with water. A watering can with a fine rose may be used, or a purpose-built spray. In either case make sure that the implement is completely clean and contains no trace of chemicals from previous use. Simply flick the rose or spray lightly over the truss to dampen it. This is best done at the time of morning when it is just getting warm. If it is too hot you may risk scorching your plant.

Pinching out

Pinching out of side shoots is another progressive job that continues as the plant grows. It is done to ensure that as much strength and nutrient as possible go into the fruit rather than into unnecessary foliage. The side shoots come between the main stem and the leaves are plucked out between the thumb and forefinger.

Stopping

The purpose of 'stopping' a plant is to make sure that it doesn't develop more trusses than can grow and ripen during the limited ripening season. The method is to pinch out the very top of the stem, leaving one leaf above the highest truss. In the case of indoor plants this will be the sixth or seventh truss, but with outdoor plants with a shorter ripening season four (or maybe five) trusses are the best you can hope for. There is an old country saying about four trusses for tomatoes and one for chutney – meaning that your last truss probably won't ripen but you will have green tomato chutney!

Ring culture

For the gardener with a greenhouse, ring culture is an alternative growing method. For this you will need a bed of gravel or clinker about 15 cm (6 in.) deep and a 25 cm (10 in.) whalehide pot with an open bottom for each plant.

Planting. Clear a circular recess in the gravel and then work in the whalehide pot so that it retains its circular shape and is firmly bedded. About half of the pot should be above the level of the gravel. Now fill it with good loam or John Innes No. 3 compost and plant straight into that. As some of the soil is above the gravel level it warms up more quickly, promoting the growth of the plant when it is young. As with more traditional methods, the plants should be spaced 45 cm (1 ft 6 in.) apart.

Watering and feeding. Once the plants are established, watering the gravel should provide any moisture necessary for the plants. If, however, feeding is necessary, use one of the proprietary feeds diluted with water, and apply this directly into the pot. Feeding is not normally needed until the first truss of fruit begins to develop. Warning: feeding too soon will result in all foliage and no fruit.

The bush tomato

Now for my final suggestion – the bush tomato. You might call it the lazy gardener's dream of heaven – no staking, no tying, no side shoots to remove. The only things to remember are that you need to leave more space between plants (a good 75 cm (2 ft 6 in.)) and that you must put a little straw under the fruit so that they don't lie on the soil and rot.

Bush tomato plants aren't perhaps as reliable as standard plants, but in a good summer they can produce a plentiful crop. They don't have to go into open ground – they can be grown in concrete containers, or even in an old kitchen sink if it's deep enough.

April sowings

Dwarf beans and beet go into the plot in April, as well as a small amount of purple-sprouting broccoli, kale, cabbage, celeriac and leek. Celery and celeriac seed can also be sown in April, although these must be sown in the greenhouse, to provide plants to be set out in their permanent positions in late June or early July. Melons too are sown in the greenhouse in April with a view to planting out under glass in early June.

Dwarf beans

Dwarf beans are very susceptible to a late frost so if you are in any doubt about the weather, leave them for a few more days, because nature has her own way of catching up. Plant the beans in 5–7.5 cm (2–3 in.) deep drills 5 cm (2 in.) apart and then proceed as for broad beans (see pages 34–37).

Beet

Beet is a larger and relatively easily handled seed. Sow them three at a time at 5 cm (2 in.) intervals along the drill. By sowing three at a time you give yourself an insurance policy against nature's hazards like the flea beetle, and you can afford to lose two out of every three. Calomel 4 per cent dust will take care of the root fly.

Purple-sprouting broccoli, kale, cabbage

Apart from the time of sowing, the cultivation of purple-sprouting broccoli, curly kale and the autumn and winter headed cabbages is the same as for sprouts (see page 50) except that for these three a spacing of 60 × 60 cm (2 × 2 ft) is correct but 45 × 45 cm (1 ft 6 in. × 1 ft 6 in.) is permissible on a plot of limited size. The thought of purple-sprouting broccoli and curly kale may not fill you with gastronomic delight, but these vegetables are very useful for filling the usual gap in the late season before the spring cabbage and winter cauliflower are ready.

Feeding

Feeding for all these crops is the same. The first feed is due once the young transplants get established and have put on a little growth – probably about three weeks after transplanting. Feeding then continues at intervals of, say, two to three weeks. A good handful of general fertilizer will provide roughly 85 g per square metre (3 oz per square yard), but instead of scattering the fertilizer over the entire area of ground, try placing it round the base of each individual plant. Take care not to get any on the leaves. Naturally, the feed must be hoed in.

One word of warning: don't apply any feed during the winter (approximately November to February), as the later maturing plants enjoy a rest at that time of the year and will be harmed rather than improved by feeding.

Disease

Cabbages and other brassicas can be affected by a disease called club root. The best way to avoid this is by not growing brassicas in the same soil two years in succession. Move them around a bit. Don't be put off gardening altogether by a mention of these pests and diseases. Many of them sound far worse than they really are, and most of them are not insurmountable problems. If you have healthy plants, they will fight off most attacks. Finally don't forget calomel 4 per cent dust mentioned on page 50 to prevent club root in your brassicas.

Recommended varieties

There is a wide choice of varieties of cabbage, including Pride of the Market for early maturing, or Autumn Supreme for September and early October. For a continued source of valuable vitamins in the cold winter months there is a choice of varieties, such as Christmas Drumhead, January King, Savoy Winter King, Ormskirk-Rearguard and Winter Salad. The latter can be cut in December and stored in a cool place for up to four or five weeks; it is also a good variety for chopping and eating raw in salads.

Leeks, celery and celeriac

Leeks, celery and celeriac are some of the optional extras that are not in our basic kitchen garden plot but none the less are certainly worth consideration. Sow these seeds in the greenhouse following the instructions on the seed packets, or in the case of celery and celeriac it may be more convenient to buy seedlings from the nurseryman. Leeks can be sown in the open ground, following the method stated for onions.

Transplanting leeks

When the time comes to transplant, the leeks should be about 12–15 cm (5–6 in.) high. Before putting them into the soil it is advisable to trim 2.5–5 cm (1–2 in.) off their tips, as this will help to prevent them from flopping over like wilting lilies which may cause the tips to become trapped in the soil. You will need a 10 cm (4 in.) deep drill for the leeks,

Transplanting leeks

in fact a mini-trench. Make holes at the bottom of the trench with a dibber, about 15 cm (6 in.) apart – the depth of the hole is determined by the amount of leek that was previously buried (normally speaking, that is the white part of the leek). Plant the leeks in the holes and firm them in. This 10 cm (4 in.) drill, or mini-trench, serves a double purpose. In the first place, it helps with the watering since a deep trench remains moist for longer. Secondly, as the plant grows, the earth can be teased into the trench to keep the edible part of the leek nicely covered and white, or 'blanched'.

Transplanting celery

Celery has certain similarities in its transplanting to leeks. This time you will need a trench 45 cm (18 in.) deep and 45 cm (18 in.) wide (hard labour again) into which you fork a layer of manure. Place the celery plants in the trench about 30 cm (12 in.) apart. As with the leeks the soil from the sides

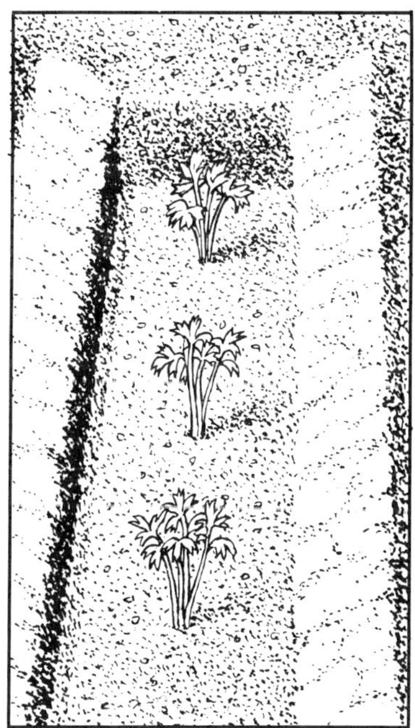

Transplanting celery

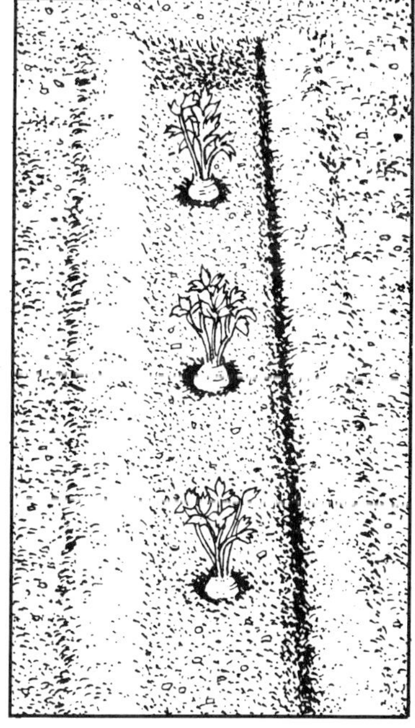

Transplanting celeriac

of the trench should be gently teased in as the plant gets bigger in order to keep the celery blanched.

Experts claim that this type of celery is far superior to the self-blanching type, but for simplicity of cultivation, the self-blanching celery should not be ignored. For this type you do not need to dig a trench – simply plant it about 23 cm (9 in.) apart each way in holes, the depth of the hole being determined by the previous growing depth of the celery. The self-blanching process is due to the fact that the plants are placed close together, thereby excluding the light, and of course it is the light which makes the plant turn green. Self-blanching celery is a crop which therefore needs a fairly large area to be successful.

A single row of the crop will simply not blanch itself. It needs the proximity of neighbours on all sides to blot out the light, and therefore produce the 'blanch'. It needs a lot of room so it has not been used on our kitchen garden plot, although there is nothing to stop you planting some if you have sufficient space.

Transplanting celeriac

Celeriac requires a slightly different planting out technique. Draw a flat-bottomed drill about 5 cm (2 in.) deep. Plant as celery, the flat drill allowing the bulbous growth to develop easily.

Celery, leeks and celeriac will all benefit from plenty of water. They should not be teased with water; plentiful but infrequent is the rule.

Melons

Melons, like tomatoes, deserve to be in this section of the book because although they are undeniably fruits, they are grown – usually with difficulty! – in the vegetable plot. It would be very nice to have a 3 × 1.5 m (10 × 5 ft) frame to grow them in, but most gardeners will use cloches. I'm afraid there's no way of avoiding this particular expense if you are going to grow melons.

Sowing

The one simple part of the job is sowing the seed. Fill a 10 cm (4 in.) pot with a good loam mixture of John Innes No. 1 compost and sow one seed to a pot. (Incidentally, the seeds are astonishingly small for a fruit that is going to grow to such a size.) Cover the seed, water with a fine rose and cover the pots yet again with a glass and newspaper until the shoots start peeping through. Minimum temperature for this is 13°C (55°F).

Potting on

It may be beneficial to pot on from the original 10 cm (4 in.) pot to a 20 cm (8 in.) pot before putting the plant into the garden. This will allow you to keep the plant indoors for a little longer than you had intended if the warm weather is slow to arrive and there will be no check in the growth while you are waiting for the weather to oblige.

Planting out

When the plants are ready to go into the garden, space them out 125 cm (4 ft) apart. It is a good idea to raise the plot about 5 cm (2 in.) to prevent water collecting round the root of the stem, as this may cause canker.

Pinching out

From here on the process is a wee bit complicated, so if you have got a neighbour who is already expert at growing melons see if you can nip round to his garden to watch and learn as he tackles each stage. Then nip back to your own garden and carry out the same process before you have forgotten how to do it! (See illustration, page 66.)

As soon as the young plants have established themselves you must pinch out the tips, leaving the two well-formed leaves. From here two laterals will develop. Once these laterals have reached seven leaves, again pinch out the tips. What are known as sub-laterals will now form from each of the leaf joints. These sub-laterals should be stopped when they have five leaves each.

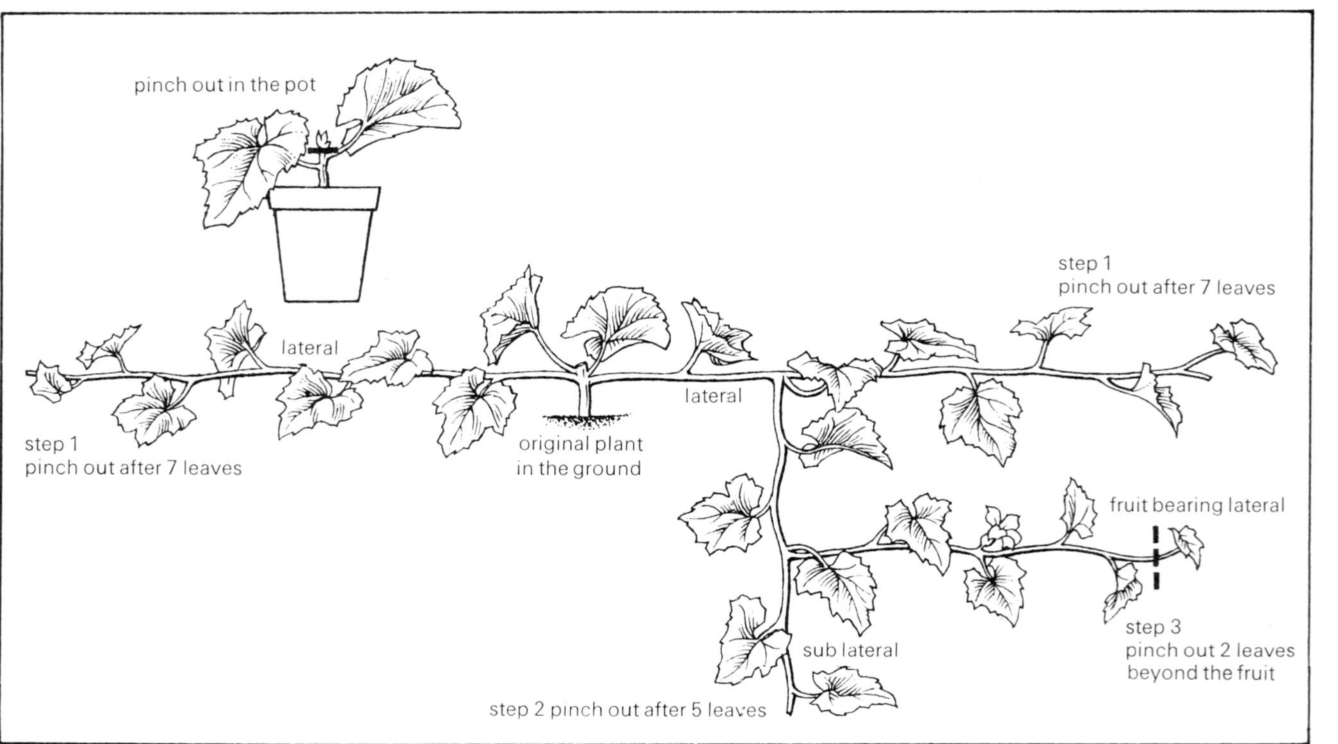

Pinching out melons

Note: Only 1 sub-lateral and 1 fruit-bearing lateral are shown here for the sake of clarity

Yet more laterals will now form. These will be the fruit-bearing ones and they should be allowed to develop until there are two leaves beyond the fruit.

Pollinating

Next you will have to lend a hand to Mother Nature, because your frame or cloches will probably keep out the bees that normally help with pollination.

First, you will need to learn the difference between the male and female flower. The female flower is easier to identify because just below the flower itself there will be a little ball-shaped protuberance which is the beginning of your melon. If it isn't there, you're looking at a male flower. Carefully take off a male flower. Then pull back the petals of the female flower to expose the stigma and transfer the pollen from the male stigma to the female stigma by applying

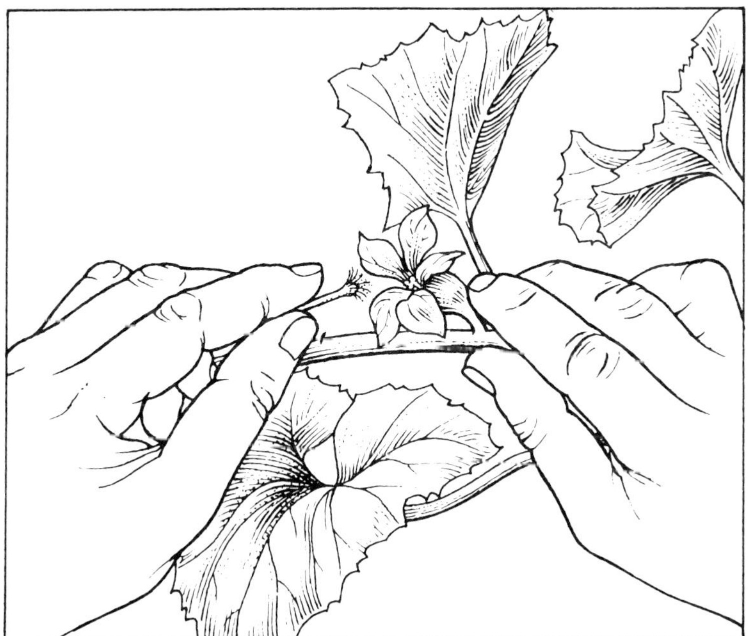

It can't all be left to the birds and bees! Pollination by hand involves lightly touching the female stigma with the male stigma

about half a dozen light touches. Once this job is done you can start looking forward to a crop of lovely melons.

Mind you, don't reckon on getting a fruit from every female flower, because you will need to reduce the number to a maximum of four per plant once the melons are clearly developing. There is one important thing to remember here – you must aim to retain four fruits of roughly the same size, in fact identical size if possible. It is no use keeping one lovely big one and three small ones because the big one will be quite disgustingly greedy, taking most of the nutrients from the soil for itself and depriving the three smaller ones to such an extent that they will probably just wither away.

Feeding and watering

A light application of a liquid feed when the fruits are well formed will help them to grow.

You must keep the soil moist at all times but don't over-water. Every time you use the watering can make sure there is a fine rose on it. It's a good idea to use tepid water, and please do the watering either in the morning or the early evening to avoid any possibility of scorching.

Further tips

A tile or some sort of board placed under each fruit will prevent any possibility of rotting.

If a long hot spell turns up it is advisable to give your cloches or frame a light shading with a lime wash or some appropriate product from your local garden shop.

5

The summer months

May sowings

The weather should be getting warmer in May, making it possible to plant cauliflower seeds and also the 'fruity' vegetables, marrows, courgettes and cucumbers. In your kitchen garden plot, aim to have one plant only of the latter three. They will provide considerable produce for two, but if you want to keep the neighbourhood supplied with marrows then simply plant a few more seeds.

In mid-May the real hard work begins if you have set your heart on a fine crop of runner beans. As you are hammering in the stakes, just remember what a mouthwatering summer vegetable the runner bean is.

Cauliflowers

The cauliflower is probably the most tricky to grow of all the brassicas. It is more demanding in terms of the attention it needs, though when you think of the great variety of tasty dishes based on the cauliflower perhaps you won't be deterred.

Sowing and transplanting

Sow the seeds in late April or early May. When it comes to transplanting you will need very well prepared soil, well dug and with plenty of humus (compost or manure), as this is a plant that heartily dislikes a check at any stage of its growth. The young seedlings don't want to stay too long in the seed bed either – transplant when they are 10–13 cm (4–5 in.) high. Spacing is 45 cm (18 in.) apart for the summer or early autumn varieties, 60 cm (2 ft) apart for the winter kind.

Cauliflower is more prone to root fly than any of the other brassicas, but there is a simple way to get over this problem. Mix a small quantity of calomel 4 per cent dust with water – quite a thin mixture will do – then dip the root of each seedling in the mixture before putting it in the ground. As ever, make sure the roots are well firmed in.

Hoeing, feeding and watering

The summer and early autumn varieties need regular hoeing and an occasional feed. Most of all, the roots must be kept moist. On the other hand, over-wintering cauliflowers should not be given too much water or too much fertilizer in the early stages, because that will bring them on too quickly. Regular hoeing is still the rule, but the main feed should not be applied until, say, late February, or when the plant is showing signs of new growth.

Varieties

Try Beacon for late September, Barrier Reef for October and Manly for late October use. West Marsh Early should be ready in February and March, Snow White is another one for March and there is Thanet for April cutting.

Marrows, courgettes and cucumbers

The cucurbits – that's a nice word to drop casually into the conversation. In fact it's the group word for courgettes, cucumbers and marrows. The cultivation of all three is exactly the same, which simplifies things quite a bit. The one aspect I am going to omit is greenhouse cucumbers, because that is a very extensive subject in itself.

Indoor-sown crops

Sowing. The starting-point with the seeds can, of course, be indoors, either in the warmth of your own home in a nice light place or in a greenhouse. Sowing time is late April or early May and the plants should be ready to go into the garden in June.

A 7.5–10 cm (3–4 in.) pot will do fine for the first stage. Now fill the pot with John Innes No. 1 compost to just below the rim, not forgetting the bits of broken clay or small stones to help with the drainage. Firm down a little with your thumbs. Then put three seeds into the pot, placing them with the sharp end or side in as opposed to putting them down flat. Cover over with more John Innes so that the pot is full pretty nearly to the top, because the watering is going to push the level down. Water with a fine rose. Then cover the pots with a sheet of glass, plus a sheet of newspaper on top of the glass. The newspaper will have to be removed as soon as the shoots start coming through, or you will finish up with long, feeble, spindly young plants that are no use at all. Keep the soil moist at all times and keep the glass on top of the pot. This combination of moisture and glass will help to provide a very localized humid climate, ideal for the initial growth of the young seedlings.

Thinning. When the plants are about 2.5 cm (1 in.) or so high and the seed leaves are formed, thin down to one plant, retaining the best-looking one of the three.

Transplanting. When transplanting time arrives (when the plants are 13 cm (5 in.) or so high) don't forget to allow three or four days for hardening off. Keep the plants out-of-doors, day and night, for that period (a sheltered corner is ideal), before taking them out of the pots and putting them into the alien environment of the open soil. Do not be tempted to skip this hardening off stage of cultivation. It would be a great pity, after all that initial care and attention to set those young plants back to a stage where you might as well have planted seeds straight into the soil.

Outdoor-sown crops

A circular drill

If you have nowhere to keep pots indoors you can sow your seeds straight into the garden. The right time in this case is May to June. Make a circular drill, a shallow depression about 13–15 cm (5–6 in.) across and 4–5 cm (1½–2 in.) deep with a nice flat bottom. The seeds are put in 5 cm (2 in.) apart round the drill, that is, in a circle, with one in the middle for luck. Cover the drill with earth and gently firm down. When the plants are about 7.5 cm (3 in.) high, choose and retain the strongest one and pull out the remainder.

Additional tips

In the case of cucumbers it is possible to save a little space by growing them up canes with just one plant to each cane. Some tying may be necessary during growth to encourage the climbing habit. In the case of marrows and courgettes you may prefer to choose the bush variety so that they don't spread and interfere with neighbouring crops.

Pumpkins

A fruit grown in the same way as the marrow and courgette is the pumpkin. It may sound a bit exotic, but nevertheless it grows very easily in most parts of Britain, and pumpkins certainly look impressive. Our kitchen garden pumpkin plant produced one fruit weighing in at 25 kg (55 lb).

Runner beans

Runner beans are, of course, the pride of many a gardener, not only for their ultimate tasty produce but also for the beautiful red flowers that make this plant a decorative addition to any garden. As a matter of fact, they were first grown for their floral beauty rather than for their edible produce.

Staking

Staking can be done in various ways, but whichever method you use the stakes should be put into the ground before you sow the seeds. In this way you will not run the risk of damaging roots and you will have a useful marking guide giving the position of the plants before they come up. These stakes must be firmly put into the ground, and driven in hard with the mallet. Later in the season the stakes will have to bear a considerable weight, particularly in the case of beans, and there could also be a good deal of wind – so hammer them in well.

The stakes should be placed in pairs about 60 cm (2 ft) apart with about 125 cm (4 ft) between the pairs. A stake is leaned towards its partner and crossed at the top. A further

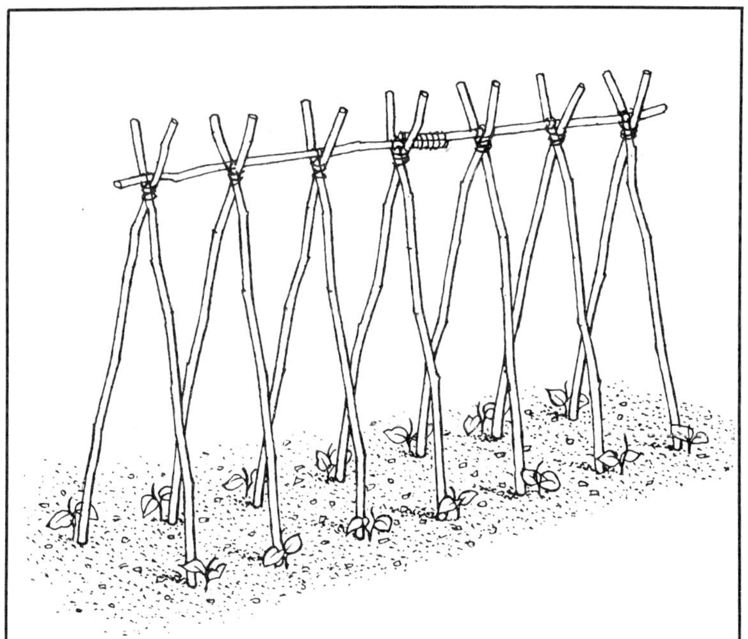

Poles are 61 cm (2 ft) apart with 1.22 m (4 ft) between the pairs.

pole is put across the pair of sticks at the point where they cross, to form a ridge like that on a ridge tent. The poles are then securely tied at the top to make a strong rigid construction.

Another method of staking is the 'wigwam' construction. Take eleven stakes, each 250 cm (8 ft) long, and space them 40–45 cm (15–18 in.) apart around a circle about 125 cm (4 ft) in diameter. The poles are then made to lean inwards to meet at the top and again securely tied off.

A third, simpler and indeed cheaper method is called the 'maypole'. Drive a pole about 250 cm (8 ft) long into the ground vertically for 60 cm (2 ft) of its length, leaving 180 cm (6 ft) above ground. Tie strings to the top of the pole, and bring the strings out to the edge of an imaginary 125 cm (4 ft) diameter circle, with the pole at the centre. Fix these strings into the ground with hooks like tent pegs. Another advantage of this method, in addition to the low cost, is that it is possible to cultivate a fast-maturing crop like lettuce in the middle of the circle, before the beans grow up the strings.

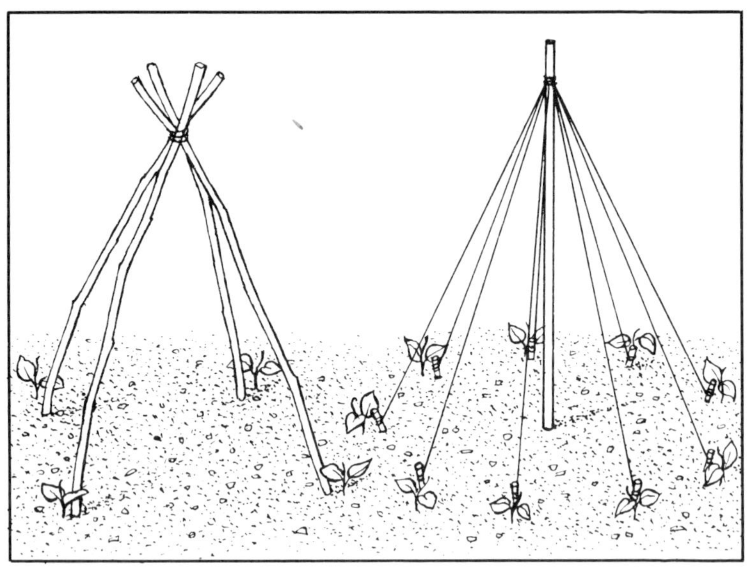

The 'wigwam' – for a smaller crop.

The 'maypole' – use string if you're short of poles.

Sowing

Sow 50mm (2 in.) apart in a drill 7.5–10cm (3–4 in.) deep and subsequently thin to 10cm (4 in.). With the Kelvedon Marvel variety it is a good idea to pinch out the tops of the plant just before the flowers open, as this will make the plants more bushy, which is just what you're after. In a really dry season this variety can give appreciably better results than the staked kind. What is more, it usually produces a crop a little earlier than its taller relation.

Growing prize runner beans

Sowing. If it's perfection you're after you must set about growing the real runner bean. You've got a fair-sized job ahead of you. Start by digging out a trench a good 45cm (18 in.) deep and getting on for 1 m (3 ft) wide to allow for a double row. Fill the bottom of the trench with a layer 10cm (4 in.) deep of manure or compost or grass cuttings or any combination of these three, bearing in mind that the grass cuttings are probably the least helpful. Cover this to a depth of 25cm (10 in.) with the soil you have already taken out of the trench, but make sure that the soil that came out last goes back first. Now leave this mixture to cook for a couple of months (you can even put your feet up if the rest of the garden will let you do so!). This means starting the job very early, say in March, in readiness for a May sowing. Just before sowing put the remainder of the top soil back into the trench cavity. By the way, if you have used grass cuttings please don't use any to which weedkiller has been applied. The weedkiller will have precisely the same effect on the beans as it had on the weeds – and I dare say you won't find that very encouraging.

Thinning. If you are growing for showing you must not only prepare the ground carefully, but also restrict the crop. When you have a stem with a mass of tiny beans just set on it they must be reduced to just two beans per stem. This is vital if you are to grow beans that are not only long but of high quality.

Final preparation. Some hints now about the final preparation of your prize product for the day of the show. Obviously, you should pick pods that are straight, even and of good quality, as well as of admiration-evoking length.

On the night before the show take an ordinary tea-cloth, soak it in cold water, wring it out and wrap one bean at a time in the cloth, rolling it over progressively until you have twelve or so beans (depending on the required number for the show) wrapped in the cloth but without touching one another. Leave them overnight wrapped up in this way and next morning when you unwrap them they will be fresh, straight, sparkling and ready for the show. Remember, even if you don't win a prize there is always one superb consolation – you can still eat them!

Maybe by now you're cringing in a corner at the thought of all this work, so I'd better let you off the hook. None of this detailed preparation is necessary for an ordinary crop of runner beans, though of course it's never wasted, even if the crop is merely aimed at the humble tureen on your table.

Catch cropping

Many gardeners under-use their plots. After taking out their early-maturing crops they leave the ground fallow until the following year. Occasionally it is a good thing to allow the ground to lie fallow. Our suggested kitchen garden plot is small, and so to make the most of it you will need to use the ground again for more crops before the end of the growing season. This method of extending the growing life of your plot is called catch cropping. Simply replant the areas left vacant by early-maturing crops with other crops that will mature before the late autumn. You can of course replant lettuces and radishes, peas, broad beans, and possibly potatoes, but you can also take the opportunity to introduce some of the more unusual vegetables to your plot.

By mid-July your plot could be looking a little bare. The broad beans will have gone, likewise most of the lettuces and radishes, the spring onions and the early potatoes, and soon the dwarf beans will be leaving an empty patch behind them. Don't leave the plot bare. Sow more seeds, and enjoy more vegetables before the season is over.

First you will need to remove all traces of the old crops, except in the case of beans and peas. Usually a thorough hoeing and raking is all the ground will need to make it ready for re-sowing. Where you are replanting after beans and peas remove only the haulm. They should be cut off at ground level, and never pulled up. Both peas and beans have small nodules on the roots which contain nitrogen and this is highly beneficial to the new seeds you are about to sow.

It is advisable when catch cropping not to plant the same crop in the same place. Move the crops around, put the lettuces in the radish bed, the radishes where the peas were and move the peas to the lettuce bed. Certain plants will draw off certain constituents in the soil, and by changing the plants around you will avoid the earth of your plot becoming deficient in any nutritional constituent through the over-planting of one particular crop. The carry-over of disease is also less likely if the crops are changed over, not only just where catch cropping is concerned, but also when considering next year's plot. Rotation of crops is a very important factor in small-scale and large-scale growing.

The seeds you put in for catch cropping will need to be the early-maturing variety since you will have to harvest them fairly soon. To start with, some of the less well-known crops (see also the chart on pages 27–30).

Kohl rabi

This is a somewhat unusual vegetable from the Continent. It tastes like a cross between cabbage and turnip. You can sow it from April until mid-July, so it is a good candidate for catch cropping. It matures in about ten to twelve weeks from sowing. Sow the seeds in 2.5 cm (1 in.) deep drills, and if you are planning more than one drill keep them 38 cm (15 in.) apart. Later thin the seedlings to 7.5 cm (3 in.) intervals.

Golden beet

This is a fast-maturing crop that can be sown as late as July. Sow in 13–25 mm ($\frac{1}{2}$–1 in.) drills, keeping the drills 30 cm (12 in.) apart. Use the method described on page 60 for ordinary beet – groups of three seeds at 5 cm (2 in.) intervals.

Salsify and scorzonera

Both these exotic-sounding plants can be sown later in the year. They have the advantage of being 'winter hardy', which means they can be left in the earth through the winter and harvested when required. Sow them in 2.5–4 cm (1–1½ in.) drills, leaving 38 cm (15 in.) between rows, and thin to about 20 cm (8 in.) between plants.

Winter radish

These are normally sown in July for harvesting from October onwards, making a marvellous addition to winter salads. Sow them in 2.5 cm (1 in.) drills, with 30 cm (12 in.) between the rows, and thin the seedlings to 7.5 cm (3 in.) between each plant. Don't forget the calomel 4 per cent dust to prevent root fly.

Cauliflower

Some varieties of cauliflower can be planted in July to produce heads in late autumn. Sow as described on page 69.

Cabbage

Another useful catch crop. July-sown cabbage usually matures in autumn. Sow as described on page 60.

Spinach

A late sowing of spinach can be extremely useful, especially if your perpetual type is suffering from constant cutting. A good variety here is Green-market. Sow in a shallow drill about 2.5 cm (1 in.) deep, and thin to 15 cm (6 in.) between individual plants.

There are of course other crops that can be sown as late as July for harvesting in the autumn. A browse through your seed catalogue will tell you which ones. Catch cropping is an important part of the vegetable growing year, so don't ignore it or you could be turning your back on some delicious late autumn crops.

6

Harvesting for storing

It is hard today to imagine that there was a time when you couldn't rely on the cold cabinet at the grocer's for vegetables that were 'fresh-frozen'. But even in pre-freezer days there were still methods of storing vegetables so that you could enjoy many of the late summer vegetables all winter long.

The garden will go on producing some vegetables in one form or another throughout the winter. It is possible, for instance, to harvest up to six different crops in January. Nevertheless, it is helpful to be able to supplement these winter vegetables with some of those grown in the autumn and then stored. Not only does this give you more variety, it also makes certain vegetables readily available at a time when they are at their most expensive in the shops.

What vegetables to store

Some root crops will store through the late autumn until well past Christmas, and the carrots and beet will certainly last into early spring. The beetroot grown on our kitchen garden plot was stored by the method described on page 81 for a whole year and was still edible. The storing process for carrots is similar to that of most root vegetables such as beet, winter radish, turnips and kohl rabi.

Good storing starts when you take the vegetables out of the ground. Great care should be taken to see that they are not bruised or damaged in any way. Any crop that has an imperfection should be used immediately in the current cooking pot and not stored for use in a future one.

The second golden rule for good storing is to lift your vegetables from the ground when the ground is as dry as possible. Wet, muddy vegetables will not store.

What you will need

You will need a wooden box for storing the vegetables. One approximately 60 × 45 × 60 cm (2 ft × 18 in. × 2 ft) should be adequate, but for larger storings use a larger box. If you intend to store only a few vegetables, then the box can easily be subdivided with a simple partition to make it possible to store two vegetables in one container.

You will also need a storage medium, that is, the stuff into which you will be putting your vegetables to keep them over winter. It can be either peat or sand, but peat is recommended. It should be just moist enough to be really effective, not too wet, not too dry. To test for this condition, take a handful of peat and squeeze it in the hand – if moisture comes out between the fingers then the peat is too wet. If the peat falls apart in the hand then it is too dry. It should just hold together. The peat needs to be in this just moist condition in order to protect the crops you will be storing. If the peat is too wet it could cause the vegetables to sprout or go mouldy, and if it is too dry it will cause them to shrivel up. The right consistency of peat will give you 'fresh' tasting vegetables all through the winter.

Place a 5 cm (2 in.) layer of peat at the bottom of your storing box. If the slats at the bottom of your box are wide apart you will need to line the bottom of the box with a layer of newspaper. Now you have a bed in which to store your carrots or other vegetables.

Storing carrots

First, cut the green tops off the carrot, cutting them just where the green part joins the orange part. Lay them on the peat, point to point, with a small gap, say 6 mm ($\frac{1}{4}$ in.) between each one. It is important that the carrots should not

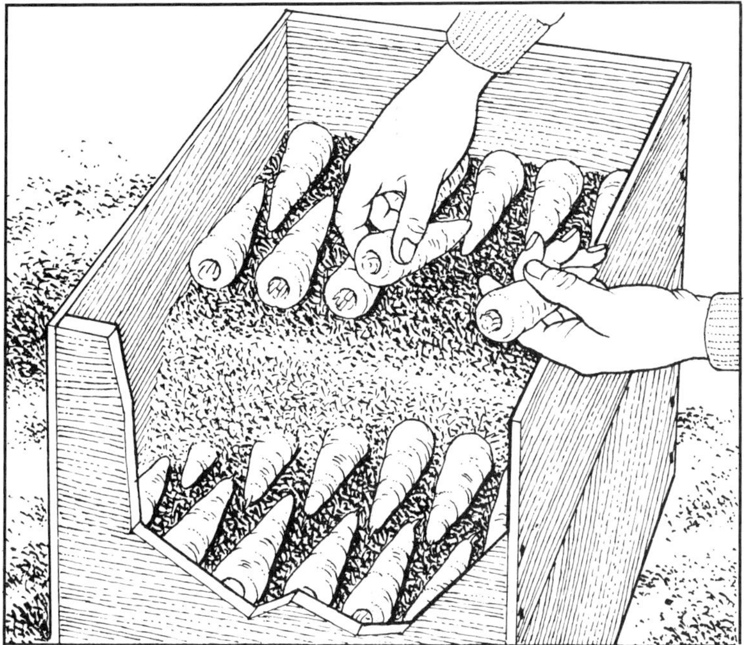

Storing carrots

touch each other, nor be in any danger of rolling towards each other and then touching. This layer of carrots will need to be covered with peat before the next layer is put in, and it is important that the carrots should be kept apart vertically as well as laterally. When the box is full of alternate layers of carrots and peat, to within about 75 mm (3 in.) of the top, fill the box to the top with peat, and store it in a cool dry shed. A fair amount of frost will not harm carrots stored in this way, though if the top layer of peat becomes crackly with frost, do not disturb it but allow it to thaw out before removing the carrots you need.

Storing beetroot

Beetroot are stored in much the same way as carrots, although in the case of the beet the tops should not be cut off, but screwed off with a deft twist of the wrist.

Storing turnips, kohl rabi and winter radish

Turnips and kohl rabi should be allowed to retain about 2.5 cm (1 in.) of their stems for storing, while the winter radish should lose its top in the same way as the carrot.

Storing parsnips

One other root vegetable, the parsnip, has even fewer storage problems. It can be left *in situ* in the earth all winter and harvested as required.

Storing beans

Beans are another vegetable that can be stored, particularly the Chevrier Vert or the climbing French bean – the variety called 'Earliest of All'. The Chevrier Vert is a particularly useful bean as it can be harvested in a very young state for immediate use, or left until an intermediate stage to give young green beans, or *flageolets*, when shelled. Finally, if they are left on the plant they will ripen and dry and when shelled they will produce the dry white bean, the *haricot blanc*, for the bean pot, the *cassoulet*, or as the basis of baked beans. The climbing French bean will also produce a small dry white bean for winter storage, which can be cooked in similar ways to the *haricot blanc*. Beans can be stored in a paper bag or in a glass jar with an airtight lid.

Storing onions, shallots and garlic

Onions are an ideal plant for storing – ask anyone who has bought onions from the blue-bereted Breton onion sellers who cycle round the south of England selling their wares. Onions are not difficult to store, but it is important that they should be in a good state for storing. The tops should be shrivelled and lying over on the ground, while the bulb should be a golden brown.

Care should be exercised when lifting the onions, as with all other crops for storing. It is important that the onions should not be damaged and they should be eased out of the ground with a fork, taking care not to tear the roots. Ideally, they should be left lying on the ground for a few days to dry out fully. If the weather does not permit their drying off outdoors then take them inside and allow them to dry off under cover. Remember that although onions may look hard and solid, they will bruise as easily as apples, so handle them with care. Once the onions are dry tie them up by their foliage, either in long strings, like the Breton onions, or just in bunches of about eight, tying raffia round their foliage. Hang them up in the roof of the shed or some other cool dry place. It is possible to store them in an open shed as they are not affected by frost.

It is not essential to tie the onions into bunches. You can, if you prefer, cut the tops back to within 5 cm (2 in.) of the bulb and then store them in a string bag or sack *(not a plastic sack)* and hang it up somewhere where the air can circulate. They can even be stored on slatted shelves, as long as there is the essential circulation of air.

Shallots and garlic can be stored in the same way.

Storing celeriac and leeks

Celeriac and leeks are two other vegetables which can be stored very satisfactorily over the winter months. Both vegetables can be stored out-of-doors in trenches which you will need to dig in December when clearing out the plot in preparation for the next year's sowing. Both vegetables can in fact be left in the ground, but storing them by the trench system means that less space is needed and the ground can be cleared at the same time.

You will need a trench about 10–13 cm (4–5 in.) deep for both celeriac and leek, but the trench for the celeriac will need to be slightly wider than that for the leek. Since celeriac is a rather bulbous vegetable, the trench must also be flat-bottomed, though the leek will only need a V-shaped trench.

Having prepared a home in which to store your vegetables, you will need to prepare the vegetables themselves. The celeriac will need to lose much of its greenery. Slowly and carefully take off the greenery at the top of the bulb. As you remove the greenery, take care not to remove the leafy stems right in the middle of the plant. This, with the bulbous root, is what you will need to store over the winter. Put the

Storing celeriac and leeks

celeriac root into the flat-bottomed trench to the same level as it was in its original growing place, thus allowing the remaining bit of greenery to show through the surface. You will now know where to find your celeriac. Put the celeriac into the ground about 2.5 cm (1 in.) apart from each other. Although you are storing them in the garden, they are taking up less space than they did when they were growing.

Leeks will need to have their green parts cut down to about 10 cm (4 in.) above the white edible parts. If this is not done, the leaves could well fall over and become mildewed on the ground. This deterioration then passes down the leaves to the roots of the plant, making it inedible. Having cut off the top green, place the leeks in their trench to the same depth as they were before you took them out, leaving about 13 mm ($\frac{1}{2}$ in.) between each leek. Cover up your vegetables with the earth, making sure that their green bits show above the surface.

Storing herbs

Parsley, thyme and sage will continue in the open for some time into the winter, but if you want to store them you will need dry weather and a crop in prime condition. Cut yourself an easily manageable bunch, tie round the stalks and hang the bunch up to dry in a cool, dry, airy place. When the leaves become brittle rub them down between your forefinger and thumb, and store them in a glass jar with an air-tight lid. A screwtop jam jar is ideal, but paper bags will do in a really dry place.

Storing marrows and pumpkins

Marrows and pumpkins are the simplest of all crops to store. You can keep them almost anywhere that is dry, and they will last half the winter without any fear of deterioration. No special beds or trenches, no preparation: just keep them somewhere dry and airy and they will obligingly be there and ready whenever you want to use them.

Short storing period: cauliflowers

Brassicas are not generally considered to be good subjects for storing, particularly when it is possible to grow sprouts, kale, spinach and cabbage all the winter. Cauliflowers can be kept for a short period of time, say about a month. If they are likely to be damaged by early frost, lift them, complete with roots, and lay on a cold floor. To prolong their life even longer, wrap the roots with wet soggy newspaper, tie round well with string, and hang them upside-down from the roof of the shed or any other cool place.

7

If space is limited...

This chapter is aimed at two groups of people. First, at the diehard flower gardener to whom the thought of surrendering space to edible crops is sheer anathema. Secondly, at gardenless gardeners – those with a patio or a balcony or even a concrete backyard.

A mini-salad plot

Let's start by planning a tiny salad plot. An astonishingly wide variety of salad crops can be grown on this mini-plot, yet our flower gardener need only surrender a small section of a flower border – say 3 m (10 ft) of an average border about 1.4 m (4 ft 6 in.) wide. What's more, the crops will add to the appearance of the border rather than detract from it.

Obviously, with such a tiny area it's essential to plan very carefully in advance what you are going to grow and where you are going to put it. So do study the diagram of my suggested layout (see page 88) so that you can follow my ideas more easily.

Choice of crops

I am aiming to get nine different salad crops from this mini-plot – cucumbers, tomatoes, beetroot, carrots, lettuces, radishes, cabbages, spring onions and corn salad. (In case you don't know it, corn salad is a green-leaved plant that can be used as an alternative to lettuce. The leaves are rather like a dandelion leaf in shape.)

Planning

Let's take each crop one at a time:

1. A roughly square space is allocated for a *cucumber* plant that will grow up a stake.
2. Next to it a sizeable space is reserved for two *tomato* plants.
3. In front of the tomatoes there is room for half a row of *beetroot*. As these are slow-maturing they will be living in the soil right through the season.
4. Now comes a full row reserved for *carrots*. You can lengthen the harvesting of the carrots by lifting some of them when they are very young, small and tender, leaving the remainder in the ground quite a while longer to grow on to full size, ready for chopping up and using in, say, coleslaw. In this way you can thin without any waste.
5. The carrots are followed by a full row of *lettuce*. This is where you have a trick up your sleeve. Instead of sowing the full row all at one go, you will divide this into four separate sowings with a week or ten days between each sowing. Not only will this result in greater continuity in the supply of lettuces, it will also allow you to grow different varieties. Each sowing will, of course, be very little more than 30 cm (12 in.) long, but you can expect plenty of seedlings all the same.
6. A row of *radishes*. Break these up into four sowings at intervals of a fortnight or even more, as radishes mature quickly.
7. Three ball-head type *cabbage* plants, bought from a nursery. These won't be planted until June, so in effect this leaves space for planting out some of your early lettuces or even putting in a number of young lettuce plants bought from a nursery and planted at the earliest possible date – March, if you're lucky with the weather. These will provide you with your first lettuces of the season.

8 and 9. The final row is a dual-purpose one – *spring onions* and *corn salad*. Start by using it for spring onions. You'll probably be able to clear at least half by July and this will leave you with just the right space for the corn salad.

This compact planning of the plot leaves one space near the bottom for any other crop you fancy, or for planting out

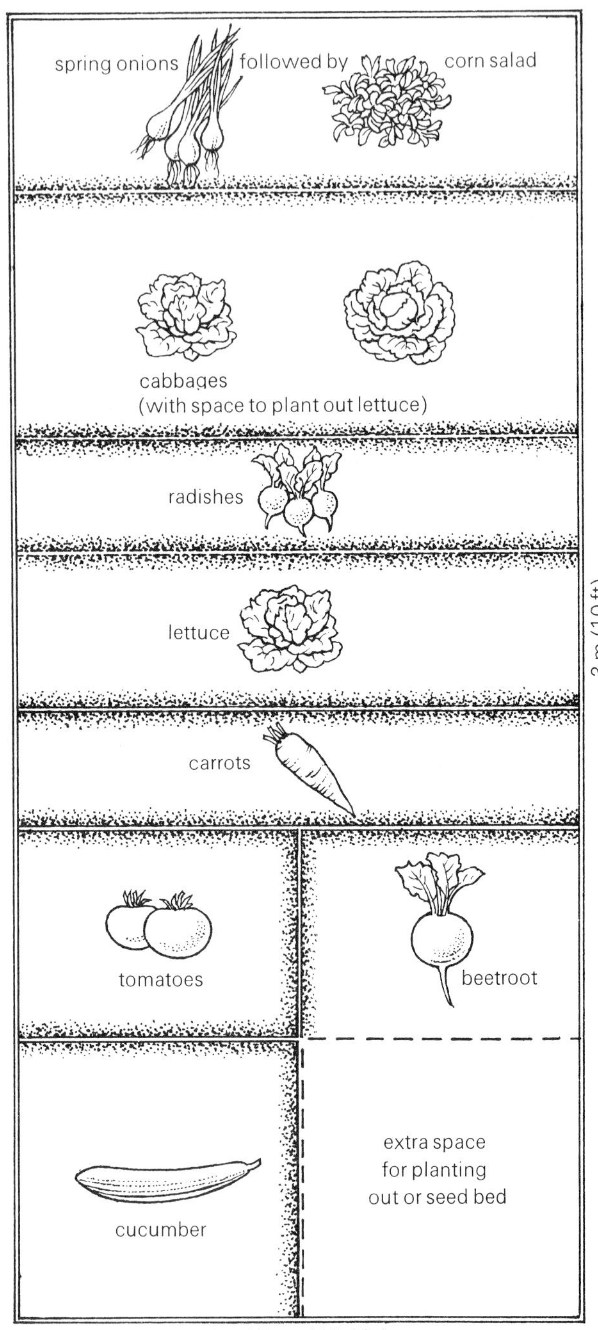

Mini salad plot

more lettuces. Your first transplant of lettuce seedlings can also go in the cucumber and tomato spaces, because they're not going to be occupied until June. What's more, you can continue to grow young lettuce round the base of the tomato plants for quite a while. They will still get plenty of light before the tomato plants are properly established.

So there is a salad plot for the flower gardener who can be persuaded to give up just a minimum of space, or for the vegetable gardener with a limited area to work on.

The gardenless gardener

If you're a gardenless gardener you've got every opportunity of growing a wide variety of crops – the only limit is the space available on your patio or balcony, in the backyard or even on the windowsill. You've got a wide choice of containers – plant pots (they'll need to be at least 25 cm (10 in.) in diameter), black polythene bags, old buckets with holes in the bottom for drainage, even old dustbins as long as they too have these essential drainage holes. Black polythene bags are generally much cheaper than the other alternatives and when filled assume the shape of the 25 cm (10 in.) pot.

Gro-bags

Gro-bags are widely available in garden shops and always have directions for their use printed on them. They are very versatile and the compost inside them is carefully prepared to give you the best results. But if cost is an important factor you will find it cheaper to use one of the other types of container.

Wooden boxes

Oblong wooden boxes can be made to fit a windowsill or to stand on the floor. If you have acquired or decided to make one, don't forget to drill some holes in the bottom for drainage. For the same reason I recommend covering the bottom with a layer of bits of broken pot or small stones. Ideally, you should fill your boxes with a good turfy loam, but ordinary soil is perfectly acceptable provided you have added about 25 per cent peat to help keep the soil open.

Filling

How you fill your boxes is very important. Not only does the filling need to be moist, it must be well packed in. To make sure of this, fill the box only half full to start with. Then push the soil firmly down, paying special attention to the edges and corners. The easiest way of finishing off the job properly is to press the soil down with a plank, or a piece of wood of similar size and shape. Make sure the soil is thoroughly moist and then repeat the process, topping up right to the rim of the box. By the time you have pressed down this second layer the soil should be about 2.5 cm (1 in.) below the top of the box.

Sowing

At this point you can bring into use the most original of all gardening tools – a kitchen spoon! This is all you need to draw the drills, and of course you can also use it for covering and firming down.

Feeding

One essential factor when you are growing anything in small containers of this kind is feeding, as with such a limited quantity of soil the plants will need extra nutrients. There is a wide variety of products on the market to do the job, and they come in quite small, inexpensive packs with full instructions.

Choice of container

Cabbages, dwarf beans, lettuces and dwarf broad beans can all be grown in pots, boxes or polythene bags. If you fancy a crop of perpetual spinach, however, it is best to use an oblong box – this is a prolific and profitable vegetable that can be picked over and over again over a period of several months. Other vegetables that thrive in wooden boxes include carrots, beetroot, radishes and spring onions.

If you decide to use cheap black polythene bags, for, say, tomatoes and cabbages, you should have no difficulty in packing in the soil so that the bag eventually assumes the normal round shape. This will give you the maximum possible area for root growth.

Just to encourage you, I must mention one of my television 'customers' who runs a pub in Marylebone High Street in the heart of London's West End. After we had exchanged pleasantries over a pint of beer recently he dragged me impatiently out on to the pavement and pointed proudly upwards. There, in a third-floor window box, were growing four magnificent tomato plants. *Nil desperandum!*

Growing fruit

Glossary

Basal cluster: The closely spaced leaves at the base of an apple or pear shoot made in the current growing season.

Blossom or fruit bud: A bud which produces flowers which will later become fruit; these buds are much fatter than those which produce leaves.

Cordon: A single straight stem on which side growths are restricted by pruning and which carries fruit spurs up its entire length.

Espalier: A central main stem with pairs of branches opposite to each other growing out at right angles on each side of the main stem.

Fan-trained: A system of training and pruning branches upward and outward from the base usually against a wall or sturdy fence so that the branches are formed into a fan shape.

Lateral: A side growth or shoot arising from a branch or leader.

Leader: The leading shoot or main growth of a branch. With a young tree the topmost growth is the leader.

Maiden: A one-year-old tree with a single straight stem. Sometimes there are side shoots and it is then known as a feathered maiden.

Root stock: The plant on which fruits are grafted or budded.

Scion: The shoot or bud of the cultivar which is grafted on, or budded on, to the root stock.

Self-fertile/self-compatible: Those cultivars of which the blossoms are capable of being fertilized with pollen from the same tree.

Self-sterile/self-incompatible: A term applied to cultivars which need to be fertilized with pollen from another cultivar before they can produce fruit.

Spur: A short growth bearing a fruit bud. Two or more spurs arising in the same growth are known as a spur system.

8

An introduction to fruit growing

In the next eight chapters I am going to concentrate on the practical aspects of fruit growing for the amateur gardener with limited space at his disposal. While many of the rules and methods of vegetable cultivation also apply to the cultivation of fruit, there is one major difference between the two – in the vegetable garden you can see and eat the results of your hard labour within the growing season, but in the fruit garden you must wait three long years before you can gather the tangible results of your first crop of tree fruits. However, there are advantages: once planted, your trees and bushes will be good for many years to come, with no annual planting, no annual digging, and none of the back-breaking attention that vegetables need. The art of growing vegetables lies in the use of the spade and the hoe; the art of fruit growing is in the use of secateurs and the pruning saw.

Until the standardization of dwarfing root stocks earlier this century, fruit tree growing was a job either for the professional or for those with a garden large enough to accommodate the traditional old apple tree and allow it to spread its branches in luxury, without detriment to the vegetables struggling for survival beneath its shade. Dwarfing root stocks were categorized at the Fruit Research Station, East Malling, Kent, originally for fruit farmers who wanted smaller trees but with a good yield – in order to avoid the time-wasting methods of fruit picking from larger trees which always involved the use of ladders. These trees grown from dwarfing root stocks are, however, ideally sized for growing in the average suburban garden. In cordon form they are small enough to grow as a dividing hedge between houses, yet they still bear a good supply of fruit. Of course the fruit can be picked quite easily from a standing position, without a ladder, and the rosiest apple is not the one that is always just out of reach. A further advantage of dwarfing stock is that one can grow two or three varieties in the space taken up by one normal-sized tree – indeed it is essential to grow more than one variety of apple or pear since they are not self-fertile.

Growing dwarf fruit trees

Dwarf fruit trees can be grown in a number of ways as well as in the traditional tree shape. Three of the most popular methods are:

1. *Cordon* where the main stem is usually trained to grow at an angle of 45° to the ground with short laterals bearing the fruit.
2. *Espalier* where the main stem is trained to grow vertically, with fruit-bearing laterals trained parallel to the ground.
3. *Fan-shaped* where the branches are trained to grow obliquely to the ground (see illustration) like the ribs of a fan as the name suggests.

You can limit the upward growth of these small trees to any convenient height – ideally about 1.7 m (6 ft). It should, of course, be emphasized that although the tree is miniaturized, the fruit is of quite normal size and each tree should bear a healthy amount – a cordon apple for instance should provide about 2.5 kg (5 lb) after its first three years in the ground.

Planning a fruit garden

The planting of bushes and trees needs to be carefully planned. Remember, whatever you plant will remain where

---

1. Cordon, grown at 45°
2. Five-tier espalier
3. Fan-trained tree

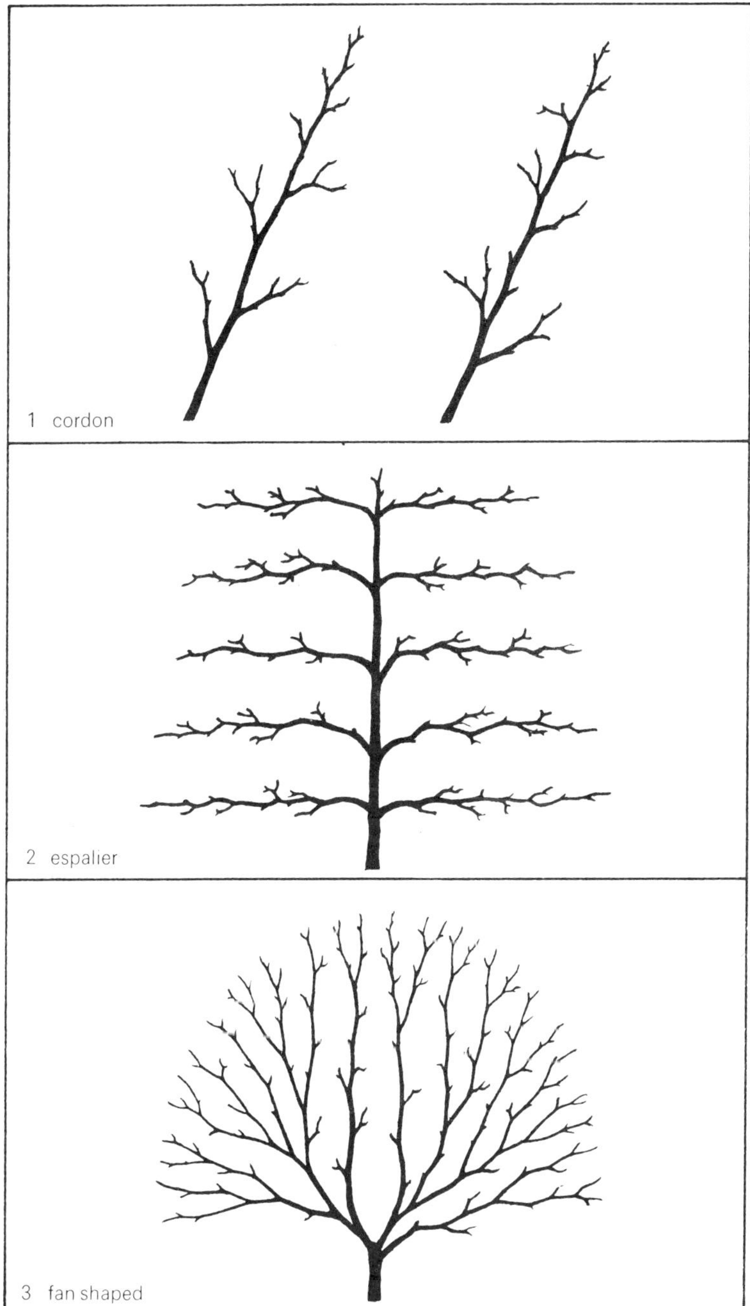
1 cordon
2 espalier
3 fan shaped

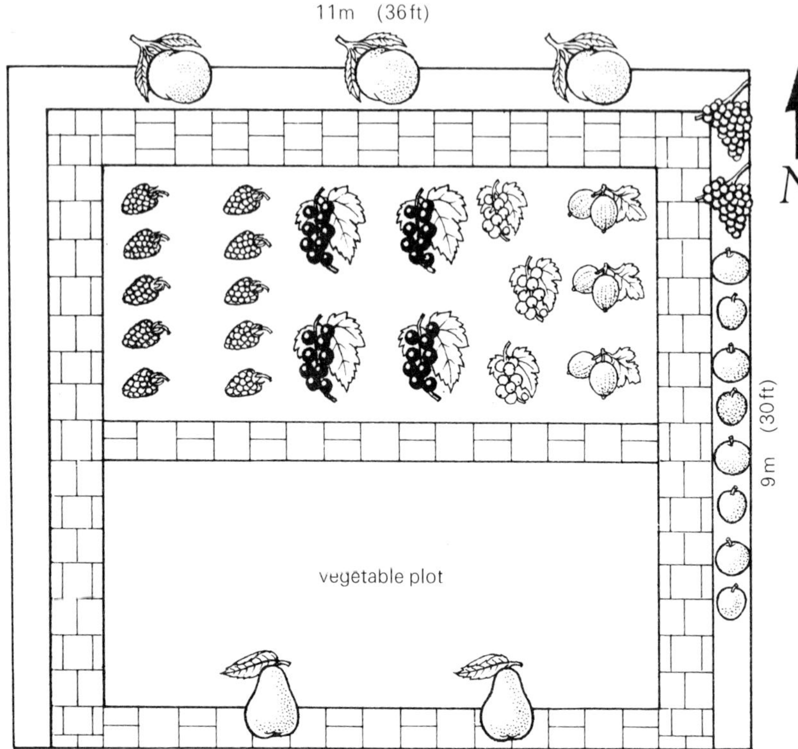

Our kitchen garden fruit plot
3 peaches, 2 pears, 8 apples, vines,
raspberries, blackcurrants, redcurrants, gooseberries

you planted it for the next twenty years or so – unlike vegetables which have to be moved each year. So give thought to the plan of your fruit garden. The same kinds of fruit should be grouped together to make spraying easier later in the year.

All fruits need sun, but some – peaches, for instance – need more than others, so they should be planted in the sunniest position. My plan, above, is based on an area 11 × 9 m (36 × 30 ft) but can be adapted to any size, smaller or larger. On this plot I have grown peaches, apples, pears, gooseberries, redcurrants, blackcurrants, raspberries, two vines and some strawberries.

On the north side (i.e. south-facing) I planted three fan-trained peach trees. Peaches are not fond of our variable climate and they need all the sun and warmth they can get, so a south-facing position is preferable, though they can be grown quite well along a sheltered west-facing wall. Peaches will also need some cosseting in the early spring to protect the blossom from frost.

On the east side (i.e. west-facing) I planted eight cordon apple trees, and put our two vines in the south-west-facing corner; on the south side, facing the peaches, I grew two espalier pears.

The centre of the fruit-growing area is devoted to the soft fruits. Three gooseberry bushes – each producing about 2.5–3 kg (5–6 lb) – three redcurrant bushes, which should have a slightly higher yield – up to about 4 kg (8 lb) each – and four blackcurrant bushes, which should also produce about 4 kg (8 lb) each. In front of the blackcurrants I planted two different types of raspberry cane – the traditional summer-fruiting variety, which can produce about 0.5 kg (1 lb) per 30 cm (12 in.) run, and the less well-known autumn-fruiting canes which start producing in September and can go on bearing fruit well into October.

The most popular soft fruit, of course, is always the strawberry, but unlike the other fruits the strawberry does not remain in the same place year after year but needs to be moved. This coincides very happily with the normal crop rotation of vegetables and for this reason strawberries are normally planted in the vegetable garden.

You can, of course, vary this layout to suit the size and orientation of your garden, and the preferences of your family.

There are many varieties of fruit to choose from. In Chapter 14 you will find lists of various recommended varieties, but a good way of finding out which types of trees and bushes are best suited to your area is to join a horticultural group and learn from the experience of others – far less painful and expensive than learning from your own. Or why not join the Royal Horticultural Society? You don't need to be an expert gardener to become a member of the RHS – and they really will give you all the advice you could possibly want no matter where you live. Their address is: Royal Horticultural Society, Vincent Square, London SW1P 2PE.

9

Groundwork for fruit growing

Tools of the trade

Once you have determined the layout of your fruit garden you will need to devote some time to choosing tools. In addition to the garden tools used for vegetables (see Chapter 1), you will need secateurs, a pruning saw and some form of spraying equipment. Various types of secateur are available at various prices, and provided it is well looked after a pair of secateurs should last for years. Spraying equipment too, comes in a number of different shapes, sizes and prices – some relatively cheap, some expensive. However, you should not normally need to spray trees or bushes in their first year of life so you can leave the purchase of a spray until the second year. (See Chapter 12 for more details.)

For the training of fan, espalier and cordon-branched trees you will need a support structure made up of strong gauge wire, tightening bolts or adjusters, wooden or concrete posts and bamboo canes. Details of how to build a support structure can be found under 'Cordon apples' in Chapter 10.

To protect your soft fruit from attack by frost and by birds you will need a fruit cage which can either be bought or built (see Chapter 11).

Preparing the ground

The ideal soil for fruit growing is well drained medium loam with a slight acid content. The amateur gardener has very

Fruit planting guide

Fruit	*Planting time*	*Distance between trees*	*Distance between rows*	*Pruning time (established trees)*	*Certification scheme (Min. of Ag.)*
Apple (cordon)	Nov–March	75–90 cm ($2\frac{1}{2}$–3 ft)	1.8 m (6 ft)	Summer	Yes
Peach (fan)	Nov–March	5.5–7.5 m (18–24 ft)		Spring	No
Pear (espalier)	Nov–March	3.5–4.5 m (12–15 ft) dependent on root stock		Summer	Yes
Blackcurrant	Oct–March	1.5–1.8 m (5–6 ft)	1.8 m (6 ft)	Autumn after fruiting	Yes
Gooseberry	Oct–March	1.2–1.5 m (4–5 ft); 30 cm (12 in.) for cordon	1.5 m (5 ft)	Winter and summer	No
Raspberry	Nov–Apr	45 cm (18 in.)	1.5–1.8 m (5–6 ft)	After fruiting and early spring	Yes
Raspberry (autumn-fruiting)	Nov–Apr	45 cm (18 in.)	1.5–1.8 m (5–6 ft)	February	Yes
Red/White currant	Oct–March	1.5 m (5 ft); 35 cm (15 in.) for cordon	1.8 m (6 ft)	Winter and summer	No
Strawberry	July–Sept	35–45 cm (15–18 in.)	75 cm (30 in.)	N/A	Yes
Vines	Oct–March	1.2–1.5 m (4–5 ft)	1.8 m (6 ft)	After leaf fall	No

little choice as to the type of soil he is blessed with, as it usually comes with the house, and many of us have far from the ideal type of soil. Nevertheless, whatever the soil there is a lot you can do to it to make it suitable for fruit growing.

Heavy soil should present few difficulties although double spit digging (see Chapter 2) will be essential in order to break up the subsoil and prevent possible drainage problems. Gravel and chalky soils will need to be well trenched and plenty of manure and organic matter should be dug in to lift the soil to the right level. Light or dry soil will also need a good supply of manure or composted material, forked well in.

You will need to double dig the entire area for soft fruits, but for tree fruits you need double dig only an area large enough and deep enough to accommodate the tree roots comfortably. Allow plenty of time for your digging; it is hard work. Always stop *before* you get tired! The site must be thoroughly prepared before planting and all perennial weeds removed. Remember your trees and bushes will remain where you have planted them for many years to come and any digging after planting will disturb the roots.

Feeding fruit trees

Fruit trees, like vegetables, need food in order to grow and a plentiful supply of manure is one of the best means of ensuring good growth. Each type of fruit has its own particular nutritional needs and what is good for one is not necessarily good for another. As a general rule, however, manure should contain phosphate, potash and nitrogen. Dig in the manure before planting the trees or bushes, and later apply dressings of bulky compost as a surface mulch round the base of the tree. Take care to keep it from touching the trunk in order to avoid rot setting in.

10

Planting tree fruits

Apples, pears, plums and other cultivars are not grown from seed. That is not to say it is impossible to grow them from seed but simply that they will not come true to type. The accepted means of propagating these trees is by budding or grafting on to a root stock. (Budding means inserting a bud of the current season's growth into a T-shaped cut on the root stock. Grafting means making a flat, sloping cut to both the root stock and stem of new growth so that they interlock, and then tying the union together with tape.) However, you don't need to go to these lengths to grow your own tree. Your local nurseryman will have adequate supplies of cultivars. Always try to buy those trees which have a Ministry of Agriculture certificate – these certified trees can be relied on to be good healthy stock, free from virus and disease and true to type.

Buying a cultivar

Trees can be bought as 'maidens', a one-year-old tree with a single straight stem, or as 'feathered maidens', a one-year-old tree with side shoots, or they can be bought up to three years old as trees already shaped by the nursery. The latter are obviously more expensive, but a lot easier for the beginner to grow.

Timing

Planting can be done any time between November and March but never when the ground is frozen nor when it is too wet. If you cannot plant your trees in their final resting place immediately, then heel them in – i.e. dig a hole or trench, put the roots of the tree into it, cover with soil and firm the soil well in.

If the weather is frosty when your trees arrive from the nursery do not unpack them. Keep them in a frost-proof outbuilding. If the roots of your tree appear dry then soak them in water for about an hour before planting.

Method of planting

When all conditions are right, dig a hole large enough to hold the roots of the tree but not so deep that the scion (the point where the stem joins the root stock) will be covered with earth; it is usually possible to see the point on the stem to which the soil came before the tree was transplanted and you can use this as a guide as to how deep to plant. Make the bottom of your hole slightly convex in shape – this will give plenty of support and also allow ample room for the roots to spread comfortably. Holding the tree in position, replace the soil by hand to start with, moving the tree up and down so that the soil slips into any gaps that may occur between the roots. Firm the soil down regularly as you fill the hole, replacing the top soil with a spade.

Cordon apples

Plant these trees 75–90 cm (2½–3 ft) apart. If you plan to grow more than one row then the rows should be kept at least 1.8 m (6 ft) apart. You will need to build a permanent support system for your cordons (see illustration), and it must be erected before you plant in order to avoid root damage. The support system is made by setting posts into the ground along a line ideally running north to south. The posts may be of iron or steel, concrete or wood, but if wooden posts are used, then they must be thoroughly impregnated with preservative and, if possible, set in concrete. Three parallel wires are then stretched tightly between the posts, the first wire (gauge 12 or 13) should be at a height of 75 cm (2½ ft) above the level of the earth, and the others (also gauge 12 or 13) should be placed at intervals of

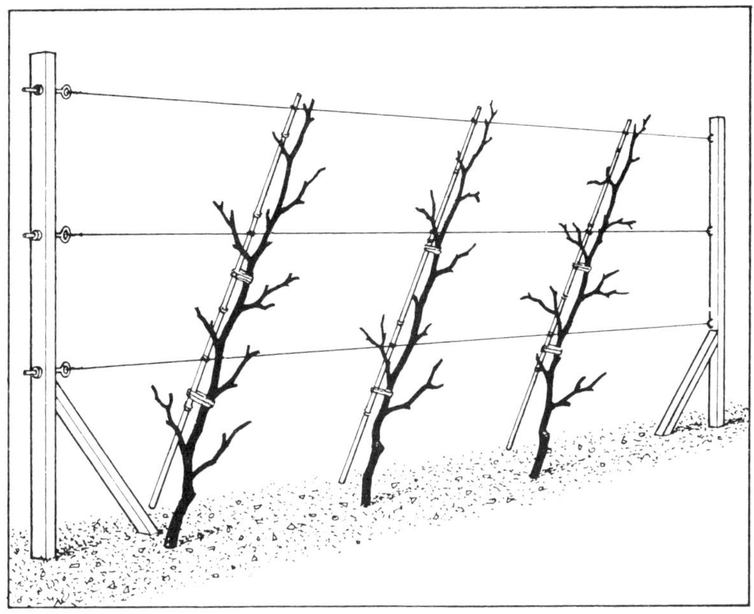

Support structure and canes for cordon apples

60 cm (2 ft). The top wire should be gauge 10. As these wires must be tight you will need to use adjusters at the end posts.

You will need bamboo canes – one for each cordon – and these should be placed at an angle of 45° to the ground, with their top ends pointing roughly north and their bottom ends attached to the bottom strainer wire. Do not put the canes in the ground as they will rot. Tie these canes on to the wires with strong string or with fine wire. Your cordon apples are going to grow up these canes, so make sure they are securely tied and examine them periodically, renewing the ties when necessary. Plant the trees with the scion uppermost and about 10 cm (4 in.) above the earth.

Initial pruning and training

If you have planted a maiden then no immediate pruning is necessary, but with a feathered maiden all side shoots more than 10 cm (4 in.) should be shortened to three buds. A word here about pruning – the be all and end all of fruit growing. Pruning is usually done 'to a bud' and buds can be difficult to identify. Sometimes they are easily recognizable as buds, but quite often they are nothing more than knobbly bits all the way along the shoot. To find out where the buds are, just run your hands gently along the branch and you'll soon feel the hidden buds.

Espalier pears

Plant espalier pears 3½–4½m (12–15ft) apart to allow the branches to spread sideways. You will need a support system similar to the one used for the cordons. It consists of support posts and horizontal wires which should be stretched 30cm (12in.) apart up the posts until the desired height is reached. Later you will need a bamboo pole fixed vertically to the wires to support the main stem of your espalier. Place the tree in the ground in a hole large enough to take its roots comfortably and cover with earth to a level 10cm (4in.) below the scion. Firm in well as you plant.

Initial pruning and training

In the maiden tree's first winter you will need to prune back to a bud lying about 5cm (2in.) above the first (bottom) wire, but make sure that there are two good buds fairly near below it – one bud facing to the left and the other to the right (see illustration). These are the buds that will form the first tier of your espalier; they will grow into branches to be trained along the bottom wire of your support frame.

In the first summer train the shoot from the top bud vertically up the bamboo pole (see illustration), but do not train the side shoots horizontally – not yet awhile. First tie them to canes at an angle of 45° to the ground, because all fruit likes to grow upward and towards the light. If one side should grow more than the other and appear to be more advanced, retard it a little by lowering the branch so that it lies in a more horizontal position with less light, and at the same time raise the weaker branch on the other side so that it gets more light and grows to the same maturity as the stronger partner. At the end of the season each of these shoots should be about 45cm (18in.) long and this is the time to lower them to their horizontal position, tied to the

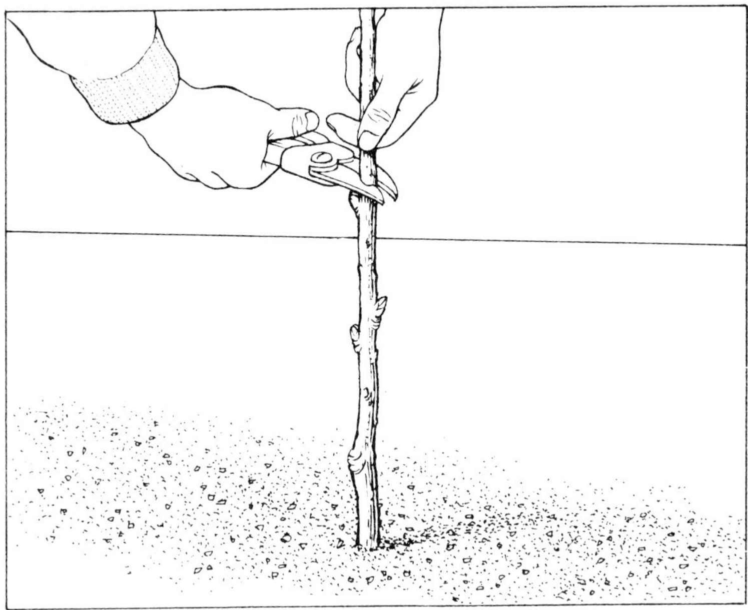

A slanting cut just above the third bud

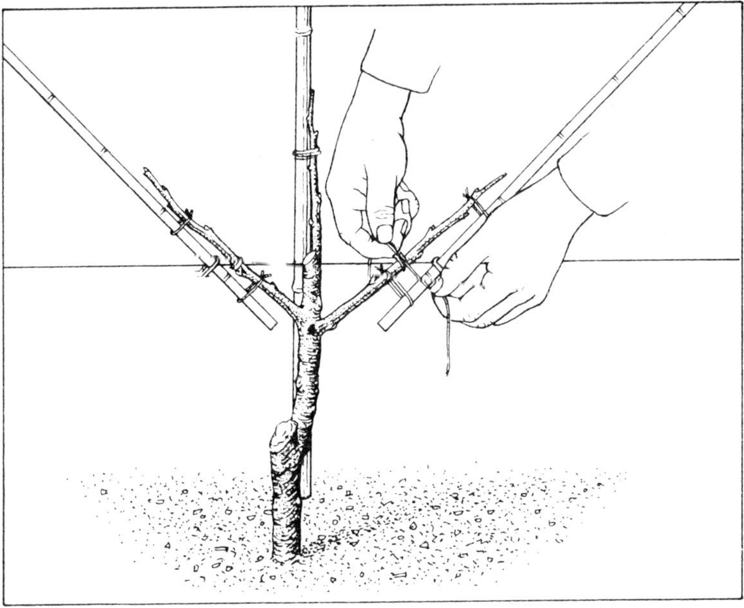

Fix canes to the wires at 45°. Tie the shoots to the canes

first level of wire. In the second year repeat the process, cutting back to a bud that is 5 cm (2 in.) above the level of the *second* wire – training two buds beneath it into shoots which will eventually form the second tier. (The above concerns initial pruning; for more detailed information on winter and summer pruning see Chapter 13.)

Fan-trained peaches

Peaches are best grown as fan-trained trees against a south-facing wall or fence, although some quite good results have been obtained from trees grown as bushes and from trees grown in the most unlikely situations – and of course we all know at least one person who claims to have grown a thriving peach tree from a stone. Unlike the case with apples, it is perfectly possible to do this and get a fairly true type but it is a very slow process.

Plant the trees 5.5–7.5 m (18–24 ft) apart in a well prepared site. Good drainage is essential for peaches so if you have any doubts about the drainage qualities of your soil, improve it by placing quantities of brick rubble covered with chopped-up turves into the base of the hole. Once again you will need a support system. Grow your fan-trained peach against a wall or strong fence, and across the wall stretch wires about 15 cm (6 in.) apart – about two brick courses. You will train your tree to bamboo canes tied at oblique angles on the horizontal wires, like the ribs of a fan (see illustration).

Initial pruning

A peach tree is more difficult to prune than an apple or pear tree. First of all, remember that the fruit is borne on the wood of *last* year's growth, and, equally important, you must be able to differentiate between a wood bud and a fruit bud. A wood bud is pointed and a fruit bud is gently rounded and plumper looking. Fruit buds never produce a shoot, so if you are looking to produce a shoot, it's no earthly good pruning back to a fruit bud – you need to go back to one of the pointed ones. Here's a useful tip: if you are ever in any doubt as to which is fruit and which is wood, cut back to

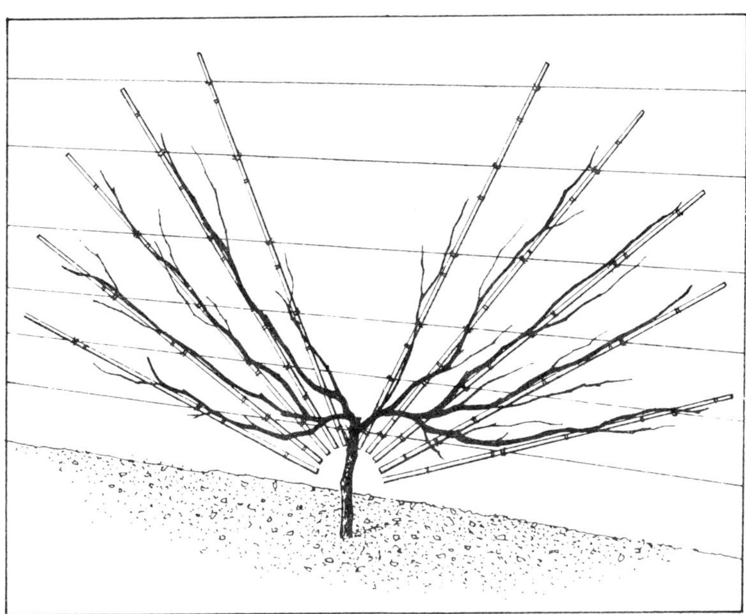

Support structure for fan training

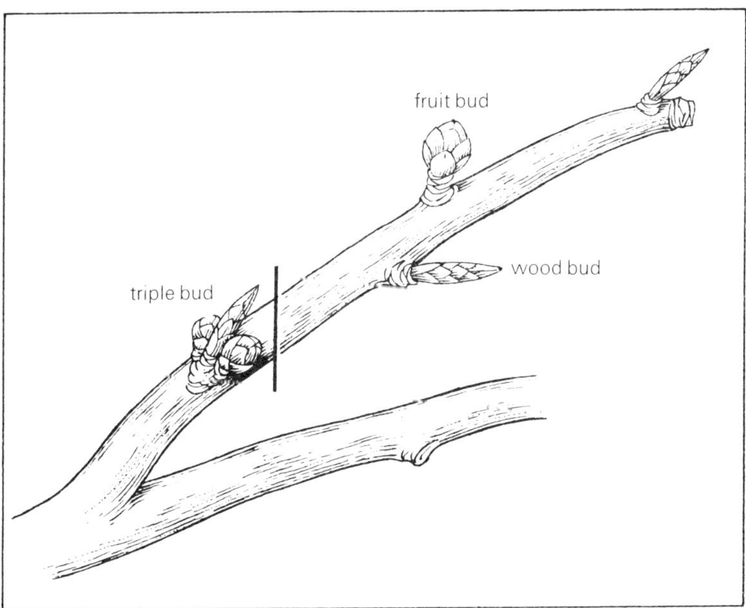

Prune to a triple bud

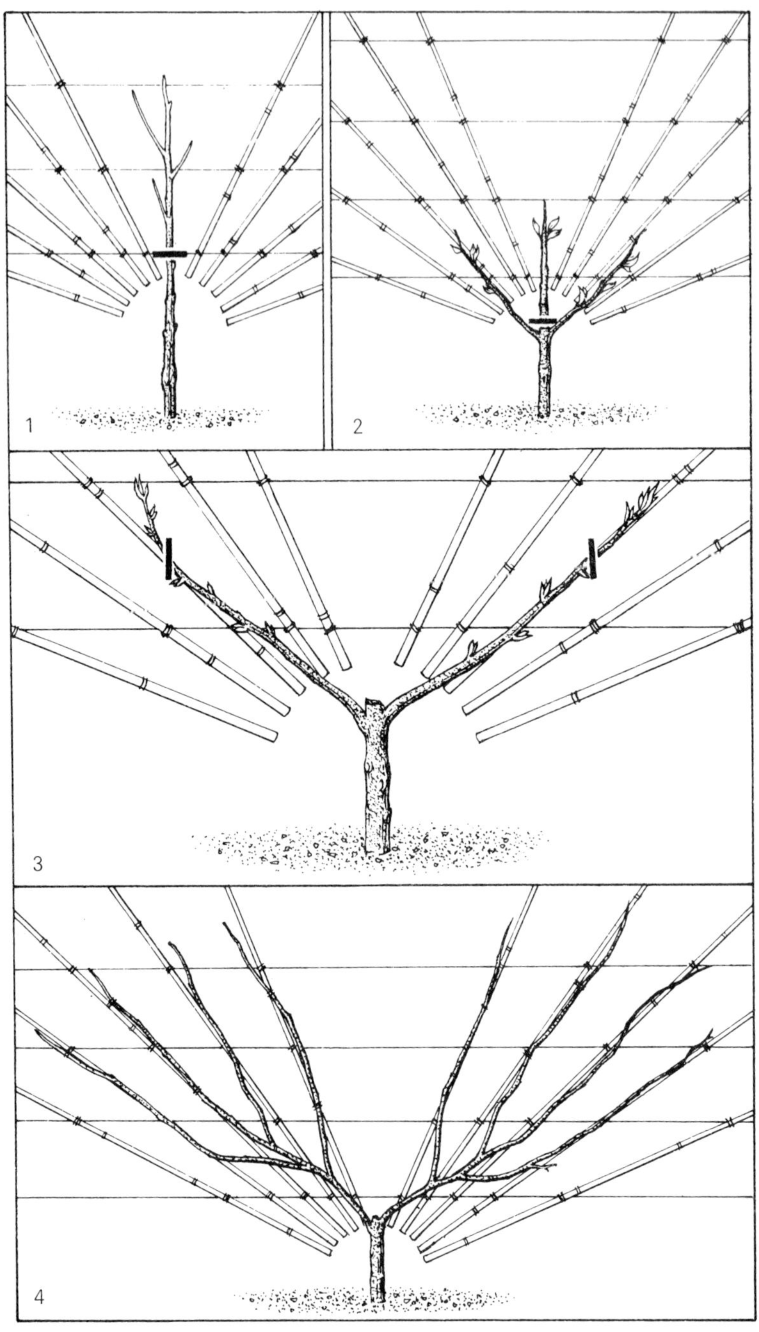
1
2
3
4

triple buds as these always consist of two fruit buds and a wood bud. That way you can't go wrong (see illustration).

In the first year after planting the maiden, cut the tree back to about 60 cm (24 in.) above the ground, if possible to a lateral or otherwise to a good wood bud with two other wood buds just below it, as with the espalier method. In the summer choose two good shoots, one on either side of the main stem about 23–30 cm (9–12 in.) above the ground. Remove all other buds except those right at the top. When the two side shoots are each about 45 cm (18 in.), tie them to canes supported on the wires at approximately 45° to the ground. If one side grows more strongly than the other, lower it slightly to curb the growth as with the espaliers. Unlike the espalier, which retained its main stem, the fan-trained tree must lose the centre stem because the branches are grown from near the ground like the struts of a fan (see illustration). Cut off the main stem carefully and dress the wound with a little bitumen tree paint.

In the following February prune back the two side shoots to a bud about 30–45 cm (12–18 in.) on your main stem. The next summer allow eight well spaced shoots to grow, two from the top of each branch; one from the bottom; and one from that bud you cut back to last winter. Rub out any superfluous buds. These new branches must be tied to the canes attached to your wire support system and trained into the fan shape that you want.

Repeat this process the following winter, cutting back all eight branches to a triple bud so that each branch is about 60–75 cm (2–2½ ft). The fan-trained peach needs careful pruning, both winter and summer, and I will go into pruning further in Chapter 13.

---

1. February (1st year) – *Prune to leave one lateral with two good buds below it*

2. June (1st year) – *Remove the spare lateral in June*

3. February (2nd year) – *Prune to an outward-facing bud at about 30–45 cm (12–18 in.)*

4. February (3rd year) – *Prune each branch to a triple bud*

11

Planting soft fruits

It is essential to protect your soft fruit from the birds, both during the winter when the bullfinches will make a meal of your fruit buds and during the ripening period when the blackbirds and thrushes will help themselves to the fruit. No matter how devoted a bird lover you are your affection will wane rapidly when you find yourself sharing your hard earned raspberries with a fat blackbird. To protect the fruit it is necessary to erect some form of netting or cage over the bushes and canes; if the fruit is grouped together you can have one large fruit cage instead of several smaller ones.

Building a fruit cage

A fruit cage construction kit can be bought from your local nursery centre – shop around to find the best prices, as they vary enormously – or if you are a keen DIY type you can build your own very simply and relatively cheaply. The structure consists of wire netting, 13–19 mm ($\frac{1}{2}$–$\frac{3}{4}$ in.) mesh, stretched between posts which may be iron, concrete or wood – if wood is used it must be thoroughly treated and buried in concrete. The top of the cage is covered with 19 mm ($\frac{3}{4}$ in.) terylene or plastic mesh draped over battens which are supported by the posts. The side netting should be removable to allow the bees to pollinate the fruit during blossom time. Bees can, in theory, get through the wire mesh but they always appear to be deterred by it.

Although you will not have any fruit to protect in the first year and will not therefore need a cage, it is prudent to allow space for it when you are planning your layout, and, if at all possible, to build the framework before you plant your soft fruit. This will avoid the possibility of damage to the roots by building it before the first bushes are planted.

Preparing the soil

As for the soil itself, the whole area will need to be double spit dug (see Chapter 2). Later, when you break up the top soil to make a fine tilth, apply a dressing of National Growmore – about 50–75 g per square metre (2–3 oz per square yard). There is no need to borrow the kitchen scales to weigh it: you will need a good sized handful, roughly speaking. A word of warning: do not be over-generous with the National Growmore. Too liberal an application will promote the growth of the bush at the expense of the fruit.

Gooseberries

These berries are fairly easily grown – not too demanding and tolerant of most conditions. They are usually grown as a bush, but can be trained as cordons or against a wall in fan-shaped form.

Plant your bush at any time during the autumn or winter when there is no frost. The bushes should be placed 1.2–1.5 m (4–5 ft) apart and planted firmly but not too deeply. (If you plant the bushes as cordons then they need to be only 30 cm (12 in.) apart.)

Dig the hole for your gooseberry bush quite generously, because it needs plenty of room for its roots to spread sideways. It should be planted to the same depth in the ground that it was before transplanting. This is not as easy to judge by eye as you might think. Use a cane or stick to make a line across the top of the hole. When you put your bush into the hole you will easily be able to see the mark on the stem left by the soil from the previous planting. When this mark reaches the same level as the stick or cane lying across the top of the hole, then the hole is deep enough.

Spread the roots out with your hands before you start filling the hole. The roots will need plenty of room to spread sideways and feed the bush. Gooseberries are a very hungry soft fruit. When the bush is steady in the ground finish filling the hole with a spade and firm in the soil well around the stem.

Once your gooseberries are planted avoid any deep digging near or around them, as this will cause root damage. Remember the roots of a gooseberry bush spread further than you think. Weeds should be kept down by shallow hoeing or by the application of a herbicide.

The shoots of a two- or three-year-old bush should be cut back about halfway to an upward and inward pointing bud (see illustration), and for two or three years thereafter the growths should be cut back to a similar length. This will promote strong branches capable of supporting heavy growths of fruit. For more details, see Chapter 13 on pruning.

During winter the ground around your bush should be carefully mulched with either farmyard manure or well rotted compost, and potash will also be required since gooseberries need this nutrient. Sulphate of potash can be applied in the spring – about 22 g per square metre ($\frac{3}{4}$ oz per square yard) – and once again you don't have to measure it on the scales, a handful will be about right. If you haven't any potash available then ashes from the bonfire are a reasonable substitute.

Redcurrants

Plant redcurrants any time between October and March during a frost-free spell, the earlier the better as a general rule. Two-year-old bushes should be placed 1.5 m (5 ft) apart. If you are contemplating more than one row, then keep the rows 1.8 m (6 ft) apart. Redcurrants can also be grown as cordons, in which case they will need to be only 38 cm (15 in.) apart, but they will need to be staked as soon as the soil has settled.

Like gooseberries, redcurrants need fairly drastic pruning. Cut back to about halfway down the shoot to a good upward

---

1. Prune as indicated
2. Prune as indicated

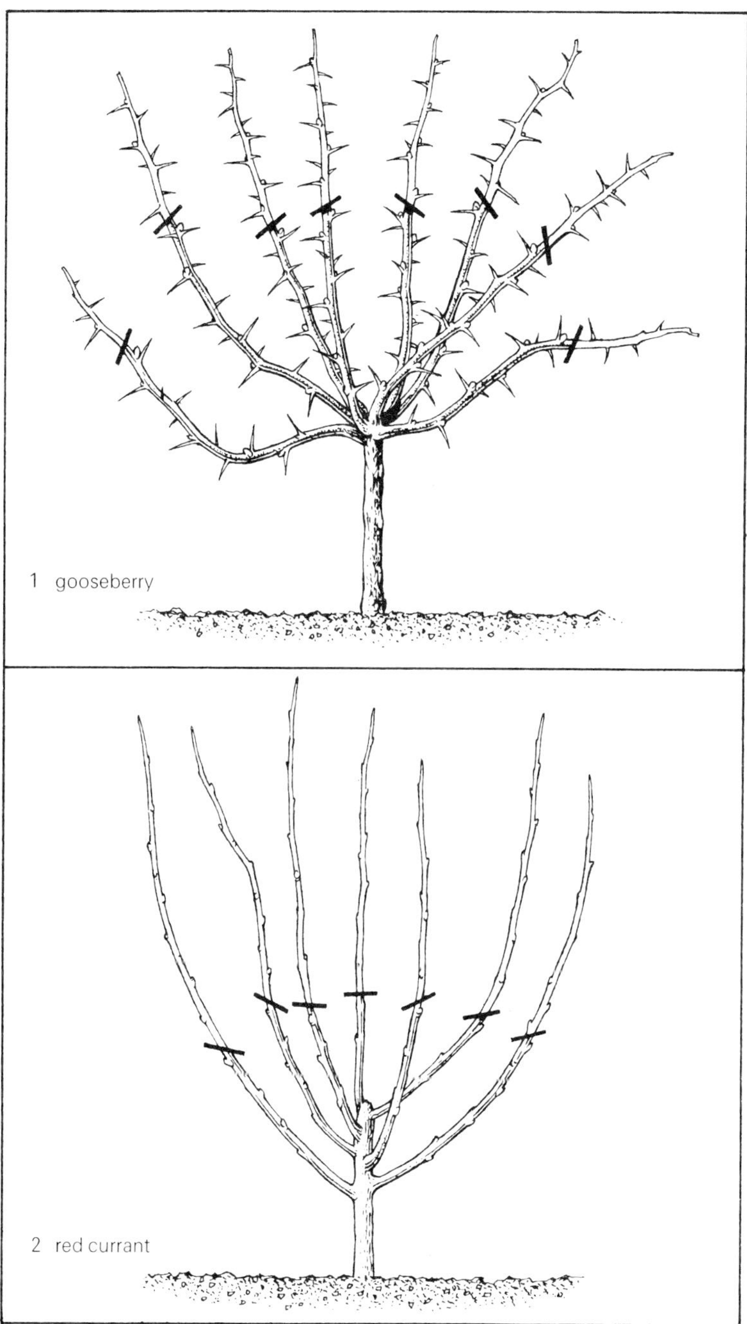
1 gooseberry
2 red currant

and outward facing bud (see illustration). The main difference between pruning redcurrants and gooseberries is that with gooseberries one cuts back to an upward and *inward* pointing bud, and with redcurrants one cuts back to an upward and *outward* pointing bud. In both cases the drastic pruning is necessary in order to strengthen the branches so that they will support the fruit.

Mulch the ground around the bush with rotted farmyard manure, taking care to prevent it from coming into contact with the main stem. Like gooseberries, redcurrants need feeding with potash in the early spring and a liberal sprinkling of bonfire ash from time to time also helps growth.

Blackcurrants

These normally prefer a sunny position but are quite tolerant of partial shade and will respond happily to a wide variety of soil types. It is best to buy two-year-old bushes with Ministry of Agriculture certificates; one-year old bushes do not carry certificates, but provided they have been propagated from healthy stock they should grow sturdily.

Plant at any time between October and March – the earlier the better – placing them about 1.5 m (5 ft) apart, and if you intend to grow more than one row then space the rows 1.8 m (6 ft) apart.

Plant the blackcurrant in a generous sized hole, and place it in the ground slightly deeper than it was in its original planting – about 7.5 cm (3 in.) deeper – and once again use the cane method to judge the depth of the hole. Fill the hole by hand to start with, firming down as you go. When the hole is filled there should be little growth above the ground. This method of planting is known as the stool system. Imagine a stool placed upside down with the seat at the level of the ground and the legs of the stool pointing upwards – this is what your blackcurrant should look like when first planted. New growth will come right from the base and this is what should be encouraged. Cut back all shoots to within 2.5 cm (1 in.) of soil level. Fruit will not form on these branches in the first year, when all the energies of the bush should be used to promote further shoots, the strongest of which will then bear fruit in the second summer after planting.

Blackcurrants need a good mulch of farmyard manure, and if this is difficult to come by, decomposed lawn mowings or other garden compost are a good substitute. Nitro chalk should be applied in March; a small handful to the square metre or yard.

Raspberries

Raspberries prefer a slightly acid soil; they don't take kindly to a high lime content. They should be sheltered from strong winds, but don't object to partial shade.

Start preparing your ground in early autumn by digging in farmyard manure or rotted down compost. Raspberries require a good supply of organic matter. The best time to plant the canes is in November although you may choose a later time provided the weather conditions are satisfactory.

These berries will need plenty of support, so before planting put a stout post at each end of the row in which you will plant your canes. The posts should be buried 50 cm (20 in.) deep in concrete or 75 cm ($2\frac{1}{2}$ ft) in soil and have about

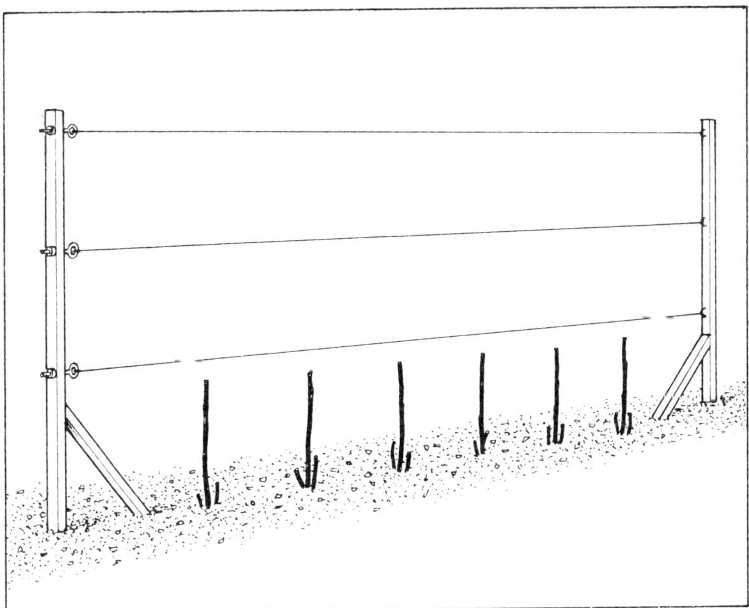

Support structure for raspberry canes

1.5 m (5 ft) showing above the ground. Stretch wires between these two posts at 60 cm, 1 m and 1.5 m (2 ft, 3½ ft and 5 ft) from the ground (see illustration). You can expect fairly vigorous growth from your raspberries, so to prevent your support structure from collapsing under the weight of the canes it is advisable to strut the end posts. As with other plants it is essential to erect the support structure before you plant the canes to avoid damage to the roots.

Dig a trench 50 cm (20 in.) wide by one spit deep in earth that has been well manured. Dig over the bottom of the trench with a fork to make sure the soil is loose and place on it a layer of well-rotted compost about 8–10 cm (3½–4 in.) thick. Dig the compost in well so that it is thoroughly mixed with earth. Raspberries need plenty of organic material to feed on, but their roots don't want to come into contact with a solid wall of compost so make sure it's well forked in.

The canes should be planted about 38–45 cm (15–18 in.) apart with about 1.8 m (6 ft) between the rows. Hold the canes in position with one hand while you fill the trench with the other. Or, better still, get someone else to hold the canes for you while you fill in the trench. The canes will look very sparse and lonely when they are first planted, but remember they are going to fill out in every direction and will need every inch of the empty space around them. When your trench is almost full, mix in a little National Growmore with the top soil as an extra feed – raspberries get very hungry.

The canes should be cut down to about 23–30 cm (9–12 in.) above the ground soon after planting. It will no doubt seem a tragedy to cut away the growth and leave nothing but a few spindly sticks poking out of the earth but you will reap the benefit later when, in the second year, your canes bear a good crop of fruit. Without the initial drastic pruning the canes would be straggly, puny and never become good fruit bearers.

Strawberries

The strawberry will give the quickest return in the shortest time of all soft fruits. Provided the ground is well prepared and you plant in July or early August, you will be able to gather your first crop by June of the following year.

For successful growth strawberry plants should be obtained from a reputable source and where possible should carry a certificate guaranteeing them to be virus-free.

As I mentioned earlier, strawberries are planted in the vegetable garden and not with the soft fruit because they are rotated in the same way as vegetables. At least one month before planting, dig into the ground a generous amount of farmyard manure or well rotted compost (about a barrow load to 6 square metres or yards). Just before planting you will need to dig in some sulphate of potash – about 15g ($\frac{1}{2}$oz) per square metre or yard – and you will also need bonemeal at about 75g (3oz) per square metre or yard. Firm the soil, rake it, and mark it out ready for planting.

The plants should be placed about 38–45cm (15–18in.) apart with the rows 75cm (30in.) apart. Make a hole large enough to take the roots of the plant and place the roots in the earth leaving the crown level with the earth. Spread the roots carefully as you plant, as strawberries need plenty of room to expand (see illustration).

Strawberries will produce not only fruit for the following year, but also the all-important runners which will give you

Planting strawberries *Gently spread out the roots*

your plants for the next season. You may leave these runners to grow in the soil and produce roots or, better still allow them to root in a pot filled with John Innes No. 1 compost. By early August, when they are well rooted, they can be removed from the parent plant and planted out.

One rule to remember: no row should remain in the ground longer than three years. At the end of this time the plants should be dug up and thrown away. Equally, propagation should not continue beyond five generations if you are to avoid virus infection.

12

Tree health

I have dealt so far with soil preparation, planting and initial pruning. These activities are all very necessary and will go a long way towards giving you a healthy crop; spraying will take you a bit further. Most pest and disease control is achieved by applying chemicals to the tree or bush at certain times, and the easiest way to apply them is with the spray.

Types of spray

There are as many different types of spray as there are diseases – from the simple and cheap to the more sophisticated and more expensive. The relatively inexpensive hand spray will be quite adequate if you have only one or two small bushes. For larger numbers of bushes or trees you will need a more effective form of spraying equipment designed to cover a larger area, such as the free-standing type which consists of a plastic container holding about 10 litres (2 gal.) with a hand pump attachment on the top and a sprayer on a length of hose. The container is filled with the appropriate chemical mixture and pumped to the required pressure, and the mixture is then released by pressing a trigger on the spray attachment. There are distinct advantages to this type of equipment, the first being that it can hold considerably more chemicals than the hand sprayer; it is also portable; and extensions to the spray attachments can easily be fitted to allow you to reach the most distant branches of your fruit tree without having to climb a ladder.

It must be stressed that all insecticides, fungicides, herbcides, and all chemicals should be kept in correctly labelled containers and *safely out of the reach of children.* Another word of warning: never use the same sprayer for weedkiller as you use for chemical spraying without washing the equipment thoroughly beforehand.

Ideally you should have two sprayers and keep one solely for weedkiller. Never pick and eat fruit after spraying – read the instructions on the container for how long you should wait before picking; never use insecticides during blossom time or you will kill off the bees and prevent pollination; and, finally, always follow the manufacturer's instructions on all chemicals, insecticides and fungicides.

Apples and pears

Apples and pears will need a fungicide to prevent scab and mildew. They should be sprayed when the leaves are sprouting, probably about the beginning of April. Spray the tree thoroughly, all over, and don't forget the underside of the leaves as well as the top. When the spray starts to drip off the leaves of the tree you will know it has had enough. Spray with fungicide every fortnight from the beginning of April until about the end of June.

Apples and pears also need a systemic insecticide to protect them against greenfly and other aphids. One spray should be sufficient for the season and you can spray with insecticide on the same day as you spray with fungicide if you wish. These two tree fruits will also need to be protected against caterpillars, and for this you will need to spray twice with a contact insecticide – once on the same day as you spray with the other two chemicals, and again later in the season, at about the end of June when the fruit will be quite well formed.

This time you are spraying to protect the fruit against the coddling moth which lays eggs on your fruit overnight. These eggs become maggots and burrow into your apples, and then will dawn that horrendous day when you take a bite out of a delicious apple from your garden and come face to face with a wriggling maggot . . . or worse, half a wriggling maggot!

Peaches

Peaches can also be affected by aphids which will attack young shoots in the spring. Spray with tar oil in December to kill off any eggs left by the aphids. In January or February you may need to spray with Bordeaux mixture to prevent peach leaf curl, a disease which appears as large blisters on the leaves.

Soft fruit

Fungicides are needed for soft fruits as well as for tree fruits. Gooseberries and blackcurrants will need three applications of fungicide at fortnightly intervals – starting at the beginning of April – to combat mildew. Redcurrants and raspberries will need spraying later in the season to prevent grey mould.

Systemic insecticide will be needed if you spot greenfly, and a contact insecticide may be necessary for your gooseberries if they come into contact with caterpillars. The saw fly caterpillar, which gathers in groups in the middle of the bush, is particularly unpleasant. This insect eats its way from the centre of the bush outwards and, in a matter of days, your gooseberry bush will be a skeleton. The saw fly caterpillar is very small at first and consequently very difficult to spot – especially as it hides itself in the centre of the bush. Examine the bush periodically for traces of the saw fly caterpillar. (If you don't mind looking like Sherlock Holmes, it's no bad thing to search with the aid of a magnifying glass.)

You don't have to nurse your trees and bushes as if they were elderly invalids – most pests and diseases can be dealt with effectively with fungicides or insecticides before they become too much of a problem. Try if you can to use only those chemicals which have been approved by the Ministry of Agriculture for amateur use. They carry the Ministry's

Chemicals Approval sign (see illustration), a large Capital A surmounted by a crown and carrying the words Agricultural Chemicals Approval Scheme.

Neglected trees and bushes

Some trees and bushes may not be in the best of health because of neglect. Very often one can buy a house and with it a garden that may not have been touched for years. Do not despair: if there are any trees or bushes in the garden it is often quite possible to restore them to healthy fruit bearers.

In the winter

Cut away all dead or diseased branches. If the tree has not been pruned for some years, there will probably be too many large branches in the centre of the tree. Be ruthless and cut them out altogether, leaving the remainder well spaced out. You will also need to cut out any smaller branches that are awkwardly placed but spread this process over three winters. Use a pruning saw for the initial heavy cutting, then pare down the cuts with a sharp knife, finishing off with a coat of bitumen tree paint over the wound. The ground beneath the tree should be thoroughly weeded, either with a herbicide or by concentrated hoeing. Once the ground is thoroughly cleared of weeds a mulch of farm manure or well-rotted compost should be laid around the trunk, taking care not to let it touch the trunk or rot may set in.

Bush fruits

If these have been neglected for any length of time it is wiser to pull them up and burn them for almost certainly they will have contracted some virus infection. However, if they have not been badly neglected, it may be possible to restore them to health by cutting out dead wood, pruning drastically, and applying a good mulch to the area round the bush.

Under-productive trees

Occasionally you come up against a tree which grows vigorously, yet produces little fruit. This can be due to a number of reasons: over-pruning in the past, the application of too much nitrogen, or simply that the tree has been grafted on to over-vigorous root stock. It is possible to check the growth of the tree by lighter pruning in winter (see page 126). Another method is to grow the trees in grass, which takes some of the nutrients and water from the ground and so deprives the tree of additional food. Where the trees may be receiving too much nitrogen, nitrogenous manures should be cut out altogether.

One other method of discouraging growth is by root pruning. This is done in November or December and is in effect cutting back the roots. A trench should be dug with a radius of about 70 cm (2–2½ ft) round the tree and the thick roots are then cut. Leave any fibrous roots as these are the feeding ones, but any downward growing roots should also be cut. Refill the hole, firming down well, and keep the tree well watered, particularly during dry spells. A young, vigorous tree could be lifted in the winter and then replanted.

13

Pruning mature tree fruits and soft fruits

Whether you are pruning tree fruits or soft fruits the main thing to remember is that trees and bushes need to be cut back or their new growth will suffer. Do not be afraid or hesitant with your secateurs. There are almost as many different ways of pruning as there are varieties of fruit and every gardener has his own particular favourite method. Perhaps the most generally used method is the one known as the modified Lorette system – a simple but effective manner to cut back a tree in order to promote new growth.

In southern England summer pruning is best done in mid-July. In the north, or in a particularly wet season, it is better to wait until August. Pruning too early in the season may encourage secondary growth which will not be able to develop sufficient strength to stand up to the rigours of the oncoming winter. If you should get secondary growth too early, then cut it back in October to one bud.

For the types of trees we have grown in our kitchen garden plot, i.e. cordon, espalier, and fan-trained trees, the only tools you should need for the modified Lorette system are secateurs and possibly a pruning saw for older growth. (For early pruning see Chapter 10.)

Cordons

To apply the modified Lorette system to your cordons you will need to prune the third leaf above the basal cluster (that is, the tight group of about five or six leaves at the base of the stem) on all the new season's growth of 23 cm (9 in.) or more. The new season's growth is easily recognizable as being fresher and greener than the old growth. Count three leaves from the basal cluster and with your secateurs cut the stem after the third leaf – i.e. leaving the third leaf on the stem (see illustration).

For existing spurs, such as those that have been pruned in earlier years, a similar system can be applied but these spurs should be pruned to only one leaf beyond the basal cluster.

The main stem, or leader, is not pruned until it reaches the height originally planned for it. Once it has passed this point it should be cut back in May each year.

Espalier

Each summer the leading upright shoot should be cut back to about 5 cm (2 in.) above the wire support, and two side buds should be trained outwards at 45° to the ground to

Prune to the third leaf above the basal cluster as indicated

form the 'arms' of the espalier – as described in detail in Chapter 10 – until sufficient tiers have been created.

Once the espalier is firmly established and is producing side shoots, the modified Lorette system should again be used for pruning. The leading shoots of each tier should not be pruned until they have reached their required length, and new growth should be kept at 45° to the ground until the autumn when it should be tied in the horizontal position.

Fan-trained peach

The pruning and early training of the maiden tree is described in Chapter 10, but many people will prefer to buy a three-year-old trained tree rather than rear their own maiden. So for them, and those who have nurtured their own fan-trained peach tree from babyhood to the third year, here are some pruning details for established fan trees.

In the third summer your trees have eight branches trained like the rib of a fan. Allow the end bud on each of these branches to grow and tie them in on to your support structure. Buds will appear on these branches, and those on the upper and lower sides should be encouraged provided that they are spaced about 10 cm (4 in.) apart. Any buds closer than this, or buds either facing the wall (or fence) or pointing directly away from it, should be rubbed out.

The new shoots should be allowed to grow only 45 cm (18 in.) long; pinch them back when they reach this length – it is on these shoots that next year's fruit will grow. Remember peaches grow only on the new wood of the previous year's growth so each year you will need replacement growth for fruit the following season.

The main work in subsequent summers will be in taking out shoots and pinching back leaves. Never allow superfluous shoots to grow: they will compete with, and take food needed for, the fruiting branches. At the base of new shoots carrying fruit you will find two or three wood buds, pointed buds as described in Chapter 10, one or two of which you should allow to grow out to form replacement shoots for the next year. Allow the terminal bud to grow out but when it has produced six leaves pinch it back to four. Each year spread this de-shooting and pinching out process over a period of about two weeks and always start at the top of the tree.

After the fruit has been picked you may train some of the shoots that have fruited to give more wall cover if there is space to be filled. Any superfluous shoots are cut out and replacement shoots tied in their place ready to fruit next year.

Raspberries

For details on early pruning of all soft fruits see Chapter 11. As soon as the fruiting is finished cut back the canes as close to the ground as possible to allow room for the new growth. Choose eight of the strongest of the new canes on each plant and train them up your support structure tying them securely to the wires and spacing them about 7.5–10 cm (3–4 in.) apart along the top wire. Towards the end of winter or in early spring you will need to give some attention to the tops of your canes – either they will need to be cut back to about 15 cm (6 in.) above the top wire, or else the tops of the canes should be bent over and tied again to the top wire. If they are left to grow, the canes could well snap under the weight of the fruit on the canes above the wire.

Blackcurrants

As the bush gets older and more established you will need to cut out about one third of the old growth each year in order to let in air and light and to stimulate new growth. You can prune just after the fruit has been picked, but if this is inconvenient it will do no harm to leave the pruning until later in the autumn. A very old and neglected bush can be restored by cutting back to within 7.5–10 cm (2–3 in.) of the ground and allowing new shoots to grow. These shoots will not bear fruit in their first summer, but should have a good yield in the following and subsequent years.

Redcurrants

In the early winter the new shoots will need to be cut back to about half their length and the laterals to two buds from the base. After four or five years it will be necessary to cut back the year's growth to about 2.5 cm (1 in.). Old branches should be cut out and new growth encouraged. At the end of June, shorten the laterals to five leaves but do not cut the leader.

Gooseberries

After five or six years the weak growth and old wood should be cut out each winter, and the main branches should be thinned, particularly if the centre of the bush is looking thick and untidy. From the third week in June the lateral shoots should be shortened to about five leaves – this will encourage fruit buds.

14

Recommended varieties and methods of storing apples

As I mentioned earlier, there are certain fruits – especially apples and pears – which, generally speaking, are self-sterile. By this I mean that the pollen from one blossom on the tree will not fertilize another blossom on the same tree. It is risky to rely on your blossom being fertilized by pollen from a neighbour's tree, so the only sure way of guaranteeing fruit is to plant more than one variety of apples and pears. There is an added advantage in that by choosing your varieties carefully you can get a continuity of fruit from early August through to the following April.

Recommended varieties

Apples

George Cave (Red) is one of the early fruiting varieties, usually producing fruit in mid-August. James Grieve takes over in September, to be followed by Lord Lambourne in late September up to mid-November. Egremont Russet should be ready to eat in October and can be stored up to December. Cox's Orange Pippin is picked late and stored up to January, as also is Golden Delicious. Ashmead Kernel is another late apple for storing, and finally Sturmer Pippin which can be left on the tree until November and stored until the following March or April.

The above are all dessert apples. If you have only a small garden it is more economical to use the limited space for dessert apples and to buy the cheaper cooking apples.

Pears

Most cultivars of pears are, like the apple, self-sterile, and so you will need a minimum of two trees and they must be compatible. (Certain types of pear are incompatible with each other, for example a Seckle will not pollinate a Williams and vice versa. So it is best to take advice when you purchase.)

Two useful varieties are Williams Bon Chretien and Conference, which between them should keep you going in pears from September through to November. If you want pears further into the winter then Seckle and Winter Nellis should store through to January.

Peaches

The peach is self-fertile, so you will need to plant only one variety. Peregrine is good for outdoor growing, fruiting in early August. Duke of York is even earlier, in mid-July, and Royal George slightly later, at the end of August. Bellegarde and Dymond are even later varieties – they produce their fruit in mid-September. There is no certification scheme as yet for peaches, so it is most important that you obtain your tree from a reputable source.

Raspberries

Most raspberries bear fruit on canes that were produced in the previous year; these are called summer fruiting varieties. There are also certain types that bear fruit on the canes of the current year's growth. These do not have as heavy a yield as the summer fruiting type, but they will nevertheless produce a good crop as late as October, perhaps November.

Malling Jewel is a good summer variety; it is also an extremely good raspberry for freezing. Malling Admiral is also summer fruiting, although later in the season. Norfolk Giant is also late, and particularly good for freezing and jam-making too. Of the autumn fruiting raspberries, both Zeva and September can be recommended.

Blackcurrants

Blackcurrants can span most of the summer months. Some, such as Boskoop Giant, are early-fruiting, while Mendip

Cross is slightly later; both these are good for freezing. Raven and Cotswold Cross are good mid-season varieties. Westwick Choice and Baldwin are both late-fruiting types and Amos Black comes very late in the season, but does not produce a heavy crop.

Gooseberries

One normally thinks of gooseberries as green in colour, but one can in fact grow red, white and yellow gooseberries. There is no certification scheme as yet for gooseberries so buy your stock from a reputable dealer.

Good varieties of the traditional green gooseberry include Keepsake, Lancer and Green Gem. Whinhams Industry is a mid-season red gooseberry, with Warrington another red, coming a little later. Whitesmith and White Lion are both good white gooseberries and Leveller a good mid-season yellow.

Redcurrants

There is no certification scheme for redcurrants, so it is essential to obtain your bushes from a reputable source. Jonkheer Van Tets is an early-fruiting variety, with Laxtons No. 1 coming a little later. Red Lake fruits in mid-season, and Rivers Late Red at the latter end of the season.

Storing apples

Many of your apples will be eaten in the winter and early spring, but the fruit does not remain on the trees all winter, just waiting to be picked as and when you want it. It has to be picked, sometimes before it is really ripe, and then carefully stored.

Apples are ready for picking when they leave the tree easily – some can be left later than others. The Sturmer Pippin, for instance, can be left until well into November provided there are no hard frosts.

Only good, sound fruit should be stored; fruit with signs of soft rot should be discarded. The apples should be carefully handled so as not to bruise them – a bruise will start soft rot which will develop into progressive rot and in time affect all the apples in the box. Hence the expression 'one rotten apple spoils the barrel'.

The three essential elements for the successful storing of apples are coolness, darkness and ventilation. An airy cellar is ideal but today few houses have cellars. A garage is a good alternative to the cellar or, failing that, the garden shed – provided it doesn't get too much sun.

Do not attempt to store apples in the loft of your house. Stored fruit needs a constant temperature of about 5.5–7°C (42–45°F) and the slightest amount of sun on the roof of your house will cause the temperature in the loft to rise dramatically, ripening the fruit before you are ready for it. Light will also speed up the ripening process so keep your apples in the dark if you want them to last the winter through.

Ventilation is most important for the storing of apples. Too much air will cause the apple to shrivel and insufficient air will cause a build-up of the ethylene gas given off by the apple. It is this gas which helps the apple to ripen and a build-up of the gas will cause the apple to ripen over-quickly. For this reason it is not advisable to store your mid-season apples with the later ones. The gas given off by the mid-season varieties will cause the later ones to ripen too early.

There are two ways of storing apples: in apple racks (or apple boxes) and in polythene bags. The apple rack is the traditional and simple method whereby you place a single layer of apples in the rack, keeping each apple apart from its neighbour so that any unseen rot will not spread between the fruit. Place the apple rack in a garage, shed or any other cool, dark, well-ventilated place. If apple racks are not readily available, you can use apple boxes. These are made of slatted wood with four corner posts and can usually be begged from a friendly greengrocer. To increase the storage life of your apples you can wrap them in specially prepared oiled tissue wraps obtainable from gardening shops or – cheaper and almost as effective – wrap them in 20 cm (8 in.) squares of newspaper.

The second method is equally simple. Take a polythene bag 40 × 30 cm (15 × 12 in.), puncture holes in it with a knitting needle to allow for ventilation and for the ethylene gas to escape, and place your apples very carefully in the bag. Never try to put more than 2 kg (5 lb) of apples in the bag – remember, the apples will be touching each other so extreme care is needed when handling them. However, if you have only a small amount in each bag, you decrease your chances of losing a large number of apples if by an unhappy chance you get soft rot spreading. Place your polythene bag of apples, unsealed, in a cool dark place and leave them to ripen. The main advantage of using the polythene bag method is that one can examine all the apples in the bag at a glance because of the transparency of the plastic.

Look at your stored fruit periodically, so as to remove any apples that may have developed rot, but always handle with care.

15

Vines

The Romans were growing vines in England nearly two thousand years ago and indeed many people still do so today. One can buy excellent wine produced from grapes grown in England – it can be found, indeed, on the wine list of an award-winning restaurant, so it can't be bad!

It is possible to grow grapes outdoors in an unsheltered position in the southern parts of Great Britain – say the parts of the country south of an imaginary line drawn from the Wash to the Pembroke Coast. And what are your chances of success? One year in three should be good, one middling, and one what the wine-maker might call a 'plonk' year. Although vines can be grown in the south in an unsheltered position, they will fare better when grown up a south-facing wall. In northern areas a south-facing wall is essential, and in these parts only the earliest varieties should be grown since they must ripen before October.

When growing and pruning vines you need to remember that you are not only caring for the fruit of the current year, but also for the shoots that will appear and grow into branches this year to become the fruiting growth of the following year.

When you buy your vine the main stem should be at least the thickness of a pencil. The main stem, incidentally, is usually referred to as the rod. Vines are tolerant of most types of soil provided the drainage is adequate. If there is even a remote chance of waterlogging then a draining system is advisable if not essential. Dig down to a depth of just over two spits and lay clinker, broken bricks or tiles to form a soakaway for water.

The Guyot system of viticulture

The best method for growing grapes in the open is the Guyot system, called after a French viticulturalist of that name. To grow grapes by the Guyot system you will need a stout support of posts and wires – a similar structure to the one used for espaliers (see illustration) – and to avoid root damage later the support system must be erected before you plant the vines.

The posts should be placed roughly 2.5–3 m (8–10 ft) apart along the row, which ideally should run north to south since this will afford most sunlight on the ripening grapes. The end posts should be sturdy, not less than 6 cm (2½ in.) in diameter and if wooden posts are used they should be treated with preservative. For added strength these end posts should be strutted. Stretch galvanized wire between these posts (gauge 12). The lowest wire should be single, the upper wires double. Twist the double wires round each other – when the vine grows it will also save you a great deal of time by obviating the need for tying in. You will also need a stout cane for each vine, to which you will tie the replacement shoot. The canes should be allowed to stand 1.8 m (6 ft) out of the ground.

Once the support structure is erected and the ground prepared, plant the vines 1.2 m (4 ft) apart. If you plan to have more than one row keep the rows 1.8 m (6 ft) apart. The best time to plant is in November or early spring. Immediately after planting you will need to cut back your vine drastically to three buds (see illustration). (It might be a wise precaution to cut back to four buds to allow for a spare.)

In the summer those three buds will have grown into shoots and you allow these three shoots to grow up your canes, at the same time rubbing out any superfluous buds. In the following autumn lay two of these shoots along the bottom wire, one to the left and one to the right (see illustration), and prune the centre one down to three buds. These three buds will produce the shoots for the next year.

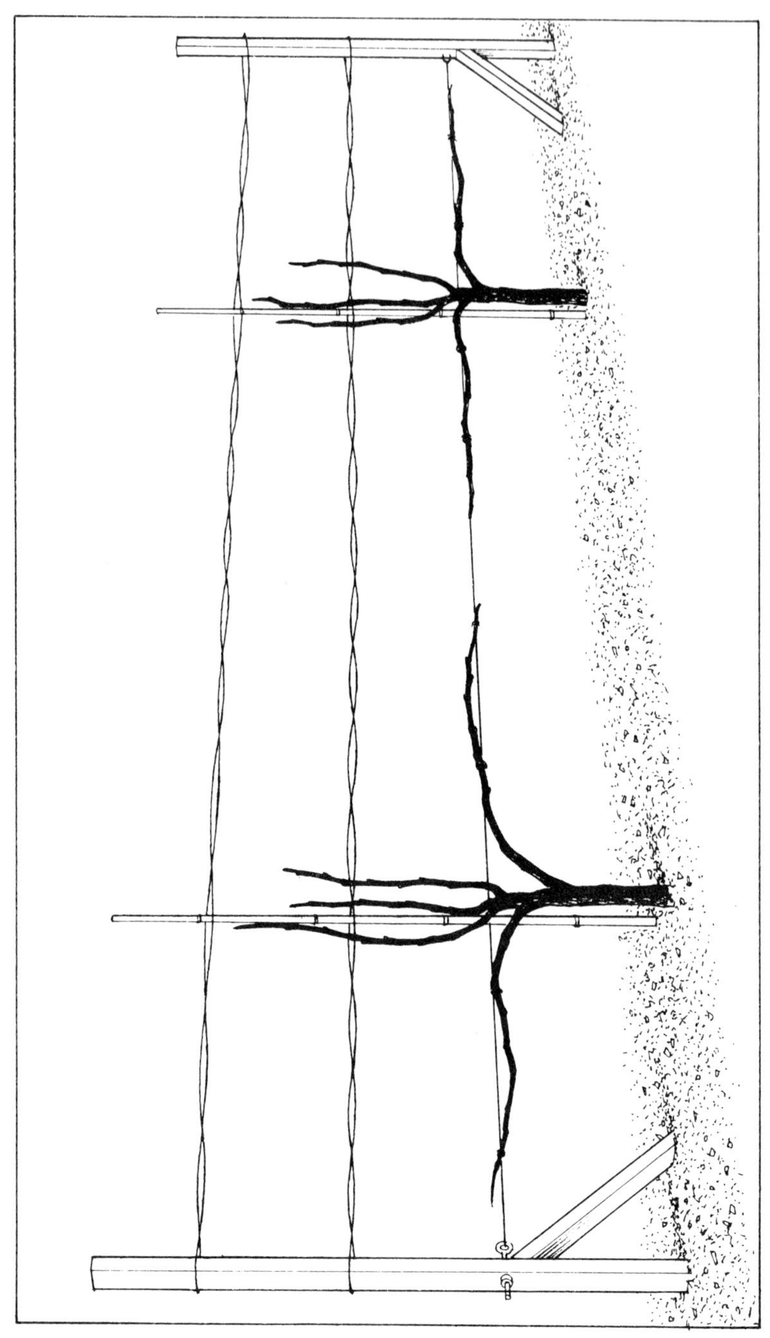

The 'arms' of the vine will form fruit-bearing laterals – but only allow at most four bunches of grapes to each vine in its first fruiting year because this will encourage good root formation. In the second fruiting year a maximum of six bunches should be allowed, whereafter the vine can fruit freely since its root formation will be firmly established.

In the autumn of the second fruiting year, as soon as possible after leaf fall, prune off the two lateral arms and all the growth that is attached to them; but be careful not to cut the replacement shoots which must be trained along the bottom wire. Prune the upright 'arm' down to three buds which of course are to become the replacement shoots for next year.

Summary of the Guyot system

1. Each autumn cut back the growth that has fruited during the year.
2. Train two new shoots along the bottom wire.
3. Cut back the centre arm to three buds to provide the shoots for next year.

Caring for your vines

It is often argued that vines require little or no feeding and that one should inhibit the growth of the wood in order to promote the growth of the grape. This may be true of the vine in the more traditional wine-growing countries of the Mediterranean with their mild climate, but with our variable weather and occasional harsh winters one should feed the vine for two reasons. First, to compensate for lack of sun and warmth and, secondly, to promote and strengthen the wood, enabling it to withstand the rigours of an English winter. Apply some National Growmore in February – a handful to the square metre or yard, plus 15 g ($\frac{1}{2}$ oz) potash. Later in the year mulch the vine with a dressing of peat or well-rotted garden compost. When the berries start to form feed your

---

Support system for the Guyot method of cultivating vines

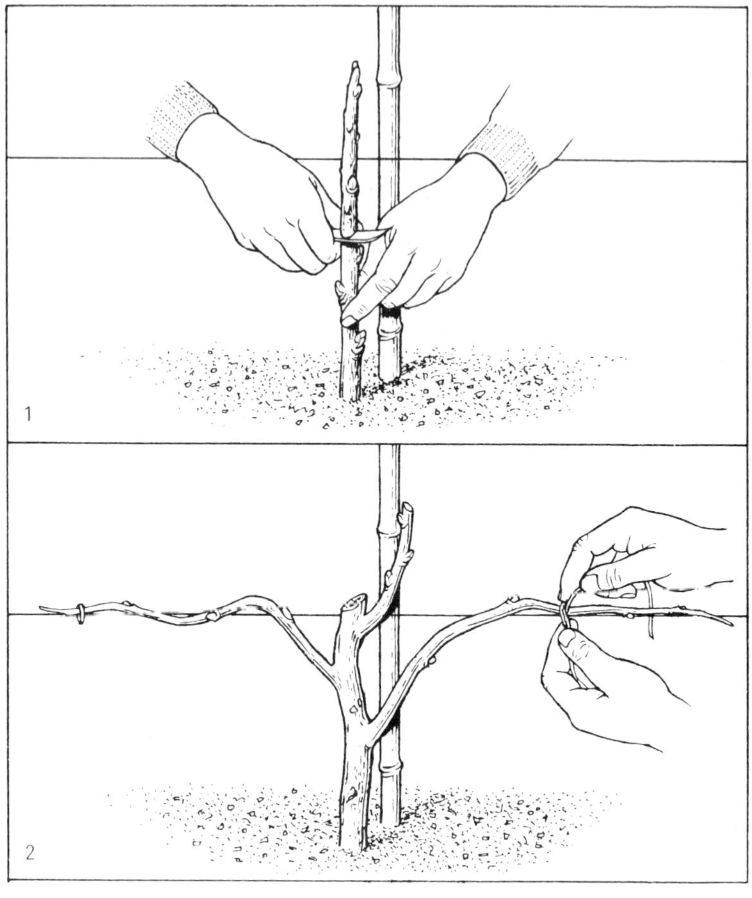

1. *Prune to three good buds*
2. *Tie the laterals to the lower wire*

vine with any recommended high potash feed at fortnightly intervals until the berries start to ripen.

Like the soft fruits your vines will be in danger from attacks by birds and wasps. The best protection you can give them is to cover them with netting from the end of August through to mid-October. If you have only one or two vines it is worthwhile protecting each bunch of grapes by putting it into a 'bag' made from nylon tights.

Spray the vines with sulphur dust before flowering, and again just after flowering when you should also spray with

Bordeaux mixture. Continue spraying with Bordeaux mixture at intervals of two to three weeks until September.

Your grapes may never reach the Château Lafîte standard, but you should produce a passable Château Back Garden – and at least you will have the satisfaction of having bent nature as far as it can be bent, for the vine is really a Mediterranean fruit.

Cooking vegetables

16

Making the most of your vegetables

Vegetables provide just about every food element we need: proteins and fats and carbohydrates, vitamins, mineral salts, roughage – you name it, and a gardener can grow it!

Unfortunately a lot of good gardening effort is ruined by indifferent cooking, so before going on to discuss recipes for individual vegetables let me offer a few basic rules. And let me start by saying that the best advice any would-be vegetable cook can be given is the same that Victorian mammas gave their daughters about sex when they launched them on to a social life: 'Don't – but if you must, do it as little as possible.' In other words, vegetables, especially freshly gathered home-grown ones, are best eaten raw. Not only do they taste better and look prettier, but they put their stores of vitamins and minerals into you, instead of down the drain with the cooking water. And there are very few vegetables that you can't eat raw.

Cooking vegetables

Those that must be cooked, however, (potatoes, for example) can be kept at their best if they aren't over-prepared. Peeling is one of those kitchen jobs that waste food, time, and a cook's energy. The merest scrubbing is all most of 'em need (I use a large nailbrush) and then you can cook them in the oven or on the hob. I much prefer baking myself, and that doesn't mean that you always have to have potatoes, for example, baked in their jackets, good as they are, or roasted in a lot of fat. Use foil to cook your vegetables: slice them, and put them in the middle of a sheet of foil with seasoning, a little butter (or margarine), or no fat at all if you want to cut down the calories, parcel it up firmly, but not too tightly (you need room inside the parcel to let the steam circulate!) and bake in a moderately hot oven, Regulo 5–6/190–200°C/ 375–400°F. Depending on the thickness of the pieces, it takes from half an hour to an hour. This method can give you baked mashed potatoes, or baked scalloped potatoes, or baked steamed potatoes – and it saves fuel, too, if you have the oven on anyway. Use it also for carrots or turnips or marrows, especially baby marrows (courgettes) or any vegetable you'd usually boil.

When it comes to leafy vegetables, however, you can't so easily use the oven. But you still don't have to boil the living daylights out of the poor things, in the classic boarding-house landlady's fashion. Shred finely first of all, or if it's a cauliflower or such, break into small flowerets. Then steam them. I use a colander over a saucepan – no need to buy fancy special pots – and cook just till they're bite tender. Spinach you can cook in butter (cabbage too, come to that) with a minimum of water. I give delicious recipes for spinach on pages 163 and 173.

Now back to basic principles. Let's consider the worst method of all, when it comes to calories, but one of the nicest when it comes to taste. Deep frying. Marvellous for courgettes and onions as well as the obvious potatoes. Slice the vegetables into bite-sized pieces, wash, make sure they're well dried after washing and then dip first in seasoned beaten egg, then in seasoned flour or coarse ground oatmeal, or even crushed cornflakes if that's what you fancy. Shake off the excess, and fry in a deep pan when the oil is smoking hot. Drain well, and eat right away. Deep-fried foods sag a bit if they're kept waiting.

Seasoning

What about the best seasonings for vegetables? There's more to life than salt and pepper – even coarse sea salt and freshly-ground black pepper, both of which I swear by because the taste difference is indescribable. Until you've tried them, you won't know how boring or dreary ordinary table salt and ground white pepper are! You also need herbs and spices. Some people are very hidebound about what goes with what, always following rules. But you don't have to! Cloves are great with apple pie, but try them with puréed turnips too. Nutmeg goes naturally on top of a milk pudding, and even more naturally with potatoes. Try baby ones fried whole in butter and sprinkled with nutmeg. About nine million calories, but the taste is fabulous.

When it comes to herbs, freshly-chopped ones are always best. To add to those from the garden, I grow a lot on the kitchen windowsill. You can never grow too many; if you get a heavy crop, keep extra supplies in polythene bags in the fridge (or freeze whole leaves). Crush them before you open the bag, and you've got it ready chopped. I used this method for mint, basil, marjoram and thyme. I know I said there are no rules about what goes with what, but let me just offer a few suggestions: try basil with any tomato dish; thyme in a salad dressing; and marjoram with cabbage. They make an enormous taste difference!

Do remember that all vegetables can be enhanced with clever additions. Like almonds fried in butter and mixed with cauliflower or broccoli. And butter-fried breadcrumbs tossed over puréed turnips or potatoes, and grilled for a final fancy touch.

Cooking spaghetti marrow

In this chapter, as well as talking about these basic principles, I would like to tell you how to cook a most exciting and exotic vegetable – spaghetti marrow. I always knew the stuff grew on trees, if only the truth were known. Easy to cook: just weight it with a glass plate in a big saucepan, so it stays well under water, and boil it whole for around forty-five minutes to an hour, depending on size. It will feel springy when it's done. Then the tricky part. Slit it in half lengthways and scoop out the seeds. Then scrape it out of its shell, and fork it up, as though you were scratching it. It will go into long green strings – that's how it got its name. I like it served with a rich tomato sauce and a sprinkle of parmesan cheese, or you can serve it hot with melted butter and salt and pepper, or with chopped bacon, or chopped fish, or cold with an oil-and-vinegar dressing. Any way you'd serve real spaghetti, in fact! Very filling, not as fattening as real spaghetti, and it tastes great.

Ingredients for tomato sauce Serves 6

Metric	*Imperial*
25 g butter or 1 tbsp oil	1 oz butter or 1 tbsp oil
1 large chopped onion	1 large chopped onion
1.25–1.5 kg fresh, skinned, chopped tomatoes	3 lb fresh, skinned, chopped tomatoes
Brown sugar; basil; sage; salt; pepper (to taste)	Brown sugar; basil; sage; salt; pepper (to taste)

Melt butter or heat oil, cook onion till transparent, add tomatoes, sugar, herbs and seasoning. Simmer till rich and dark in colour – one hour at least.

17

Onion, pea and bean recipes

In this chapter I go on to two of the most staple vegetables. Onions and pulses – the edible seeds of leguminous plants according to the dictionary, peas 'n' beans according to us.

Onions are, of all vegetables, the most indispensable. There are very few savoury dishes that don't need them and they're also a splendid vegetable in their own right. They're high in carbohydrate and vitamin C and mineral salts, especially potassium and calcium – and they have been said to give protection against heart disease! That's not proved, though, but their taste is. So try them baked in their jackets, just like potatoes and eaten with butter, or stuffed with a herby breadcrumb mixture, or of course deep-fried in rings, or simply braised.

Peas and beans are also versatile (put them in soups and stews and salads) and are as well an important source of protein, mineral salts and some vitamins. There are areas of the world where people live on virtually nothing else. Most people cook only the peas and throw away the pods. But do remember you can cook the pods, especially when they're young, with a ham-bone, a few root vegetables for added flavour (onions and turnips) and seasoning. Cook for a couple of hours, take out the bone, put the rest into a blender, and you've got a great pea soup.

Peas

Anyway, here is a method with peas that really is delectable – even better than the classic peas with mint. Take small onions, the cocktail size (and if you peel them under water your eyes won't leak – a useful tip, that), and toss them in a butter and oil mixture at the bottom of a heavy pan. I always use a little oil with butter to prevent the butter burning. Olive oil when I can afford it, ordinary vegetable oil when I can't. They'll go a little transparent after a few minutes. Then add a little sugar, a bunch of fresh parsley (tied in a little bundle so that you can remove it easily afterwards), salt and pepper, a little hot water and the shelled peas. Then put a small quartered lettuce on top, lid it tightly and leave it all to cook on a low heat for about a quarter of an hour. Longer if the peas are a bit elderly. Serve it with the quartered lettuce arranged round the edge, and add a little more melted butter.

Beans

To cook runner beans, you need only to steam them and serve them tossed in a simple oil dressing – olive oil seasoned with sea salt, black pepper and garlic. They're smashing cold, too, with a vinaigrette sauce. Broad beans can be treated the same way – though they're best eaten raw when they're very small – or tossed in a light béchamel sauce when they're getting more mature.

Ingredients for béchamel sauce Serves 6–8

Metric	*Imperial*
90 g butter	3 oz butter
4 heaped tbsp plain flour	4 heaped tbsp plain flour
875 ml milk	$1\frac{1}{2}$ pt milk
Nutmeg; salt; pepper	Nutmeg; salt; pepper

Melt the butter, stir in flour to a thick paste, then add seasoned milk slowly, stirring all the time. Cook till the mixture is thick and smooth and the flour is completely cooked. Pour over 1 kg (2 lb) cooked shelled beans.

Vegetable pâté

This recipe uses last year's beans – the Chevriers Verts or small white haricot beans dried and stored at the end of the growing season. It's a vegetable pâté. It's elegant enough to be the first course at a dinner party, if you are still able to afford to give dinner parties, that is, or great for the family. I used 500g (1lb) of beans together with a large onion, 350g ($\frac{3}{4}$lb) of mushrooms, and assorted seasonings – in this case lemon thyme, garlic, salt and pepper, celery seed and some oil for cooking.

I soaked the beans overnight and then cooked them in well-flavoured vegetable stock until they were soft. If they pop when you blow on 'em, they're cooked. This takes from one to one and a half hours depending on the size of the beans, the bigger ones needing longer. While that was happening, I fried the chopped onion in one pan, and drained off the excess oil, and then did the same with the mushrooms in another pan. If you use the same pan, you get them all the same colour – which spoils the look of the finished dish. The onions should be crisp and very brown.

Next, the mixing – the fun part, this. Put the drained beans into a bowl and mush them up with a masher. If you want a very smooth pâté, use the blender. I prefer the slightly rougher texture you get by mashing. Next, add the cooked chopped mushrooms. They, of course, will blacken a good deal, and they're going to colour the beans quite a bit. Save some of the mushrooms for the finish. Next, in go most of the fried onions, some being saved for a garnish; mix it all well – this takes time, because if you're too rough you break up the mushroom and onion pieces too much, and that spoils the appearance of the finished dish. A light hand is needed in the mixing! Then season – and taste as you go. Lemon thyme, garlic, salt, pepper – and a hint of celery seed. Don't overdo them, they're spicy! If the mixture seems a little dry at this point, add melted margarine or butter to soften it. You won't need much if you cooked the beans until very soft.

Pack the mixture into a dish and strew the top with the rest of the onions and mushrooms, and press them down. Chill it well, and when you want to eat it, have lots of hot wholemeal toast ready, some butter and an appetite! It makes a good sandwich spread too, by the way. Great for packed lunches. It keeps well in the fridge.

Ingredients Serves 8–10

Metric	*Imperial*
500 g dried beans	1 lb dried beans
1 large onion	1 large onion
350 g mushrooms	$\frac{3}{4}$ lb mushrooms
Lemon thyme; garlic; salt; pepper; celery seeds	Lemon thyme; garlic; salt; pepper; celery seeds

Vegetable cassoulet

Next, a really economical and delicious dish which is very hearty eating! Once again, some dried beans and I use here both the Chevrier Vert beans and some big butter beans. Again, soak them overnight – 250 g ($\frac{1}{2}$ lb) of each. Next morning, prepare the other vegetables – and I use lots of different roots: carrots, potato, onions, parsnips, turnips and celeriac – but not kohl rabi or swede which are delicious but rather too flavourful for this dish. Now, you'll also need pearl barley – I find that 100 g (4 oz) is ample with 500 g (1 lb) of dried beans. One more stage before you assemble your dish: the stock. I use a basic vegetable stock (page 159) to which I add pepper, soy sauce (that Chinese vegetable sauce which darkens as well as seasons), a hint of Worcestershire sauce, and any herbs you happen to like. I enjoy using a *bouquet garni* mixture – you can get it as a loose mixture you strew over the vegetables, or in a bag which you take out of the dish after it's cooked. Check for seasoning – flavouring the stock is the lazy and sensible way, and you can make it quite salty with all those vegetables to take up the salt.

Layer the vegetables into your hotpot – and the more handsome the dish, the more delicious the finished result, somehow! – and add a layer of beans, mixed. Then a sprinkle of barley, and then start again – vegetables, beans, barley – until the pot is full. Then pour over the stock. I use about 1$\frac{1}{2}$ litres (3 pt), and that's a little more than you need but not to fret as it will be needed later. Put that in the oven at a low heat (Regulo 2, depending on your oven, 150°C/300°F). The slower this cooks the better it tastes. Leave it for five or six hours or even longer – but check from time to time to see if the stock needs topping up. Then take it from the oven and once more top up with a little stock.

Now the finishing touch. Take several thick slices of buttered brown toast – leftover breakfast toast is fine for this. They go on top, pushed well down to soak up the extra stock, and then you strew over the top a thick layer of grated cheese. Sprinkle a little dry mustard on for bite and put the whole dish under a hot grill and serve when it's bubbling.

This makes enough for six starving people, and some left over for tomorrow's lunch (and it reheats a treat!) though you'll need a new bread and cheese top. Serve it with runner beans, or whole green beans, or cabbage or spinach, whatever offers you the most interesting contrast.

Ingredients Serves 6–8

Metric
500 g dried beans (soaked overnight)
100 g pearl barley
Carrots; onions; green peas; potato; parsnips; turnips; celery or celeriac
1.5 litres vegetable stock
Bouquet garni
Worcestershire sauce
Soy sauce
Salt and pepper
Toast slices
Grated cheese
Mustard

Imperial
1 lb dried beans (soaked overnight)
4 oz pearl barley
Carrots; onions; green peas; potato; parsnips; turnips; celery or celeriac
3–4 pt vegetable stock
Bouquet garni
Worcestershire sauce
Soy sauce
Salt and pepper
Toast slices
Grated cheese
Mustard

Mange-tout

Beans aren't the only things you can cook in their pods. A special vegetable is mange-tout ('eat-all'). The best way with these is to string them by pinching off the tip and pulling lightly, so that the fibrous edging of the pod comes away. Then cook them for a bare ten minutes or so in melted butter. I use so much butter I ought to get the Cow-of-the-Year award, but honestly, it's unbeatable for vegetables, whatever it does to your hips. However, you can use margarine, and a low-cholesterol one at that if you are worried about this substance you get in your diet. Cholesterol, by the way, is the form of fat you get from animal foods (meat, butter, milk, eggs) and some doctors say a low-cholesterol diet, using only fats derived from vegetables (such as corn or olive oil) is better for your health because cholesterol has been implicated in some forms of heart and artery disease. However, not all doctors agree on this point, and many fear sugar far more than fat! But if you want to play safe go for vegetable oils and low-cholesterol margarine.

Now back to my mange-tout! The French cook these with a sprig of savory, but I'm not keen on it – I think this herb has a bit too powerful a taste for their delicate flavour. You can serve these as an accompanying vegetable, but I think you get more out of them eating them as a separate course in their own right. That's true of most vegetables, as a matter of fact – we in Britain tend to see vegetables always as bridesmaids, meant to hide in the shadow of the meat or fish. But, like bridesmaids, get 'em on their own, and they can be much more interesting.

Onion bread

To finish this chapter, I offer a favourite family recipe – onion bread. I use a basic pizza dough.

Ingredients for pizza dough Makes 1 dozen slices

Metric	*Imperial*
25 g fresh yeast or 12–15 g dried yeast	1 oz fresh yeast or ½ oz dried yeast
A little sugar	A little sugar
Warm water	Warm water
450 g plain flour and pinch of salt	1 lb plain flour and pinch of salt

Liquefy yeast in sugar and water. Add to flour to make a well-kneaded dough. Leave to rise to double its bulk (about ½–1 hour).

Spread the dough into a 1 cm (½ in.) thick square in a shallow oven dish and spread it with onions which have been fried till transparent in butter and oil (or, if you prefer the flavour, beef or pork dripping) and I season with whatever I fancy. I like basil, or sage or marjoram – my mood varies – and always, of course, sea salt and black pepper. Then I cook it flat and serve cut into squares, or I roll the whole thing into a sausage or swiss roll shape, cut it into rounds, leave them to prove (that is, rise again) and bake in a hot oven (Regulo 7/220°C/425°F) till they're brown and crisp. It takes about half an hour. You can sprinkle the tops with a few more fried onions mixed with poppy seed, for a crunchy finish. Eat 'em hot! Great for family suppers, smashing for parties.

18

Green vegetable recipes

Now for brassicas – the leafy vegetables. The studio kitchen looked like Kew Gardens, it was all so green! (I thought I was being grown something to wear when I first heard about them. Instead I showed how to cook them.)

Cabbage with caraway

The cabbage family have been sadly abused in this country in the past. Shades of all those horrible school dinners with their over-boiled wet cottonwool greens. So, first of all, please don't boil cabbage in slabs. It's a sin and a crime, really it is. It should be shredded very finely and steamed in a colander-in-a-saucepan steamer. Or better still, try it this way which takes five to ten minutes to prepare.

Chopped onion is cooked to a gloss in butter and a hint of oil. Now add a shredded cabbage mixed with a teaspoonful or so of caraway seeds and a hint of salt. You have to experiment to get the taste that suits you. Stir it vigorously over low heat. After a little while the natural cabbage juices will start to run. That's the trick, with cabbage and spinach – and once you've got it, you won't need any water. You can add a little, if you feel you must, and then it's safe to cover it tightly and leave it over a minuscule heat to cook. Stir it occasionally to prevent it sticking, and when it's crisp and *al dente* – rather like spaghetti – add the juice of half a lemon. If you like you can then sprinkle the cabbage with flour and stir till that's cooked – another five minutes – to make a sort of thin sauce, but do remember that adds calories! This is especially good with any rich pork dish.

Ingredients Serves 4

Butter and oil
1 chopped onion
1 chopped cabbage
Salt to taste
Caraway seeds (about 1 teaspoon)
Juice of half a lemon

Cabbage soup

If you are a devotee of Solzhenitsyn you'll probably have a mental vision of cabbage soup as unmitigated dish water used to punish political dissidents. Real Skilly. Not so. Not if you try it this way – this really sticks to the ribs.

You need one finely shredded cabbage; a medium-sized one will do. Put a largish quantity – a few tablespoonfuls – to one side, and then peel and chop a large onion and a large potato. Sauté them together in a little margarine or butter for ten minutes or so, and then add the shredded cabbage and sauté that lightly too. Then, add 425 ml ($\frac{3}{4}$ pt) of vegetable stock – and if I may digress for a moment, you can make your own just as you make meat stock, by slowly simmering together all sorts of vegetables, including leftovers, with herbs and seasoning to taste, until the vegetables are sad rags, but the stock is flavoury. Don't use onions – too flavoury – nor potatoes, which make thick stock, but all other vegetables, including trimmings, can be used. Strain it well, and use like any other stock. And, by the way, it freezes beautifully.

Now, back to our soup. Cook the vegetables slowly for about half an hour, or until the potato is soft. Then, add 425 ml ($\frac{3}{4}$ pt) of milk, season with salt (you'll need a good deal), pepper, a little marjoram, and nutmeg if you like it – I do. When it is cool, shove it in the blender. This gives you a thick, smooth and delicious cream soup. Then reheat it – don't boil, or, like all milk mixtures, it may separate. Serve it with crisp bread croûtons (I make them by baking stale bread dipped in garlicky oil in the oven, or you can fry them, and then drain them well). Garnish with the crisp raw cabbage you saved. The texture differences make it delectable.

Ingredients Serves 6–8

Metric	*Imperial*
1 medium cabbage, shredded	1 medium cabbage, shredded
1 large onion	1 large onion
1 large potato	1 large potato
Margarine	Margarine
425 ml vegetable stock	¾ pt vegetable stock
425 ml milk	¾ pt milk
Salt	Salt
Pepper	Pepper
Marjoram	Marjoram
Nutmeg	Nutmeg
Croûtons	Croûtons

Baked cabbage

After that starter you won't want cabbage again, but you will on another night, if your gardener is as gifted a cabbage grower as mine is! Try this very nutritious, cheap and not too calorific way.

You need a large cabbage, shredded and steamed but only for a short time; make sure it remains crisp. Now take 425 ml (¾ pt) of plain yoghurt and mix with it three well-beaten eggs and 170 g (6 oz) of grated cheese. Edam is very good – medium fat and melts nicely. Drain the cabbage very well – press it under a plate, and chop it even finer if necessary, and then stir it into the yoghurt mixture. Add seasoning – salt, pepper and caraway seeds if you like these – and for an exotic touch add a small handful of shredded blanched almonds. Put the mixture into a greased oven dish and sprinkle the top with brown breadcrumbs or bran mixed with extra cheese (50 g (2 oz)), dot with butter or margarine and bake in a hot oven (Regulo 6/200°C/400°F) for about half an hour, or till the top is crisp and brown. Serve it with cauliflower fritters (see page 162).

Ingredients Serves 6–8

Metric	*Imperial*
1 shredded cabbage	1 shredded cabbage
425 ml yoghurt	$\frac{3}{4}$ pt yoghurt
3 beaten eggs	3 beaten eggs
170 g grated cheese	6 oz grated cheese
Caraway; salt and pepper; shredded almonds	Caraway; salt and pepper; shredded almonds
Optional extra:	*Optional extra:*
50 g breadcrumbs or bran mixed with cheese	2 oz breadcrumbs or bran mixed with cheese
Butter or margarine	Butter or margarine

Chinese cabbage chop suey

But let's get on to the really special dish – Chinese cabbage. It's an elegant looking vegetable, so much tidier than our sprawling British versions! It's great eaten raw like lettuce – and try cooking it Chinese style.

But first of all, do your own bit of growing – bean sprouts! Moong beans (get them in an Indian or Chinese grocer) are soaked for several hours (overnight will do) and then wrapped in a towel, and put in the airing cupboard in the dark for two or three days. Shake the towel occasionally to prevent them taking root on it. Wash and eat. They're lovely raw. But in this recipe, I cook them!

Chop a Chinese cabbage very small (really bite-sized pieces) and take a big flat pan you can use on top of the cooker. You will need a really big shallow one. Put in it a little oil, and toss in the cabbage, and cook it fast, stirring like mad all the time. They call it stir-frying, the Chinese. A very accurate language. Now, you can also add other vegetables – baby corncobs, whole, and sliced mushrooms, and of course the bean sprouts, and cashew nuts, and finely sliced ginger root which adds an authentic Chinese flavour. If you want to be extra exotic, a little sliced pineapple is fun too. It can be eaten at this stage, all hot and crunchy. Lovely! But let's go on a bit. Add a little stock – chicken stock is excellent – with soy sauce to taste (soy sauce really is the authentic flavour), then bring that to the boil, and cook for three minutes, still stirring. Then add cornflour well mixed with butter. This will thicken it all a little. And there you are – your actual Chinese vegetable chop suey! Eat it alone, as a starter, or with plain grilled fish or meat.

Ingredients Serves 4–6

Metric	*Imperial*
1 chopped Chinese cabbage	1 chopped Chinese cabbage
Oil	Oil
Beansprouts; baby corncobs; sliced mushrooms; sliced green ginger root	Beansprouts; baby corncobs; sliced mushrooms; sliced green ginger root
275 ml chicken stock	½ pt chicken stock
Soy sauce (to taste)	Soy sauce (to taste)
25 g cornflour, mixed with 55 g butter	1 oz cornflour, mixed with 2 oz butter

Cauliflower fritters

Right, now fritters. This you can do with any vegetable, in fact – mushrooms, courgettes, broccoli, aubergines, thin potato slices – but it's particularly good with cauliflower. Break into neat little flowerets before cooking or you can cook the head whole, and then break it up, as you prefer. Whichever way, drain the flowers on kitchen paper – they must be dry.

Now, to my batter. I tend to judge quantities by eye, I'm afraid, but these amounts will work well, I promise you. To 250 g (½ lb) flour – I prefer wholemeal – add four tablespoons of oil. If you are concerned about having polyunsaturated oil (the sort that is said to be better for your heart) use sunflower seed or corn oil, or olive oil, which is a neutral one. Also expensive! I find corn oil excellent, myself. Now add two whole beaten eggs – or 125 g (4 oz) soya flour if you want to leave out the eggs – and a pinch of salt, and pepper. You'll need about 250 ml (½ pt) of warm water to beat this lot into a thick batter. It depends on the dryness of the flour, the size of the eggs if you use them, or the amount of soya flour. But it should be of a coating consistency. That is, if you dip a spoon into it, the batter should just coat it.

Leave the mixture in the fridge for at least half an hour – longer if you can – and then prepare to fry. I like the deep basket method. It's easier to handle. Heat the oil to just smoking – test it with a tiny drop of batter which should curl and then brown after a moment or two – and then dip each floweret into the batter, shake a little to get rid of the excess and drop in the pan. Cook till it's all brown and crispy, and serve immediately, plain, or with a little lemon juice, or perhaps a tomato sauce. Recipe for that on page 185!

This is enough for six, as a side vegetable; or if used to accompany the baked cabbage, will serve eight.

By the way, you can use the leftover batter by dropping spoonfuls into the hot oil. My children call those bobbolets – their own word – and have a passion for them.

Ingredients Serves 6–8

Metric	*Imperial*
1 large cauliflower	1 large cauliflower
250 g wholemeal flour	8 oz wholemeal flour
4 tbsp oil	4 tbsp oil
2 beaten eggs or 125 g soya flour	2 beaten eggs or 4 oz soya flour
Salt and pepper	Salt and pepper
Water to mix (about 250 ml)	Water to mix (about $\frac{1}{2}$ pt)
Oil to fry	Oil to fry

Spinach

For spinach, use the same method as in the first cabbage recipe (see page 158), but leave out the caraway seeds. Instead use nibbed almonds, if you want to be really exotic. Or use a chopped onion and then serve the spinach with a poached egg in the middle – the classic Florentine dish. A marvellous lunch!

Sprouts

What about sprouts? They can be steamed, of course – and never ever commit the dreadful sin of putting bicarbonate of soda in them to hold the colour. They may look greener but it ruins the taste. Also, cut a deep cross shape at the bottom of each sprout before steaming it – this helps to make sure the stalk is adequately cooked through. Then try one of the additions I mentioned in Chapter 16, such as blanched shredded almonds fried in butter until they're brown. Very luscious, I promise you. You can do the same with broccoli and cauliflower. You can also use chopped chestnuts with sprouts – that's a classic Christmas garnish, of course.

19

Cucumber, courgette, marrow, aubergine, pepper and pumpkin recipes

Let's start with aubergines – eggplant if you speak American rather than French. These are so beautiful that I use them, together with peppers, as a table centre in the kitchen. Just to look at. They taste good too.

You can fry them, or braise them in a white sauce or make them into fritters, but I'm going to suggest a classic dish which is totally vegetable, and in which aubergines play a triumphant part. Ratatouille. That's right – ratatouille. Almost unpronounceable, so you can call it Provençal vegetable stew if you'd rather, because that is where it comes from. Provence.

Ratatouille

Take a large glossy aubergine, and slice it – don't peel it! – and then cut it into large pieces and strew them with salt, on a cloth. After twenty minutes or so, wash the pieces carefully and drain them well. This gets rid of the hint of bitterness that sometimes comes with these fruits. While they're waiting, peel and roughly slice a couple of large onions, de-seed and chop a green pepper and a red pepper and slice two or three courgettes (baby marrows). Also, skin, peel and chop three or four large firm tomatoes. Keep the pieces big – you want them to hold their shape. Now I cook them in a way that infuriates the purists, but which I swear to you works beautifully. You don't have to do things the hard way to make them work.

Take a handsome dish – as I said before, the look of a finished meal affects the enjoyment of the food – and trickle some olive oil in the bottom. It must be olive oil for this, because of the taste. Now put in the vegetables well mixed, all higgledy-piggledy, strewing with seasoning as you go. I use salt, pepper, and lots of basil. Last of all, take slivers of whole garlic and shove them in among the vegetables. Now a last sprinkle of seasoning, a further trickle of oil, and you are ready to cook it. Honestly, that's all there is to it. No need for anything fancier. Just pop it in the oven – a moderate one (Regulo 4/350°F/180°C) – and leave it to its own devices for about an hour. The vegetable juices will start to run in the heat, and will mix with the oil and the seasoning, and the end result will be a beautiful concoction. It looks so pretty, quite apart from how it tastes. Each vegetable shows its own colour, and when you eat it you get the blended flavours. Try it with roast chicken, or a grilled sole. Or in solitary splendour, hot or cold. One of the great dishes of the world, I promise you.

Ingredients Serves 6–8

Aubergines; onions; courgettes; red and green peppers; peeled tomatoes (all chopped)
1–2 tbsp olive oil
Basil; salt; pepper; garlic

Marrows and courgettes

Now we're on to the subject of marrows, what about courgettes, which are baby marrows? I've already discussed deep frying them, but how about this? Slit largish ones lengthways, and scoop out the innards, leaving a sort of rowboat-shaped shell. (It's easiest with a small spoon.) Chop the flesh, and mix it with breadcrumbs, chopped anchovy fillets, chopped black olives, oregano and parsley to taste, plus garlic, the quantities depending on the size of the courgettes and your own taste. Use wine to moisten the breadcrumbs if you're feeling exotic, a little milk if not. Season with black pepper, pile the mixture back into the shells, and arrange on an oven dish. Trickle over them some olive oil, and bake in a moderate oven (Regulo 5/190°C/375°F) for about twenty minutes. These can be eaten hot or cold.

Ingredients for stuffed courgettes Serves 4

Metric	*Imperial*
4 courgettes (largish)	4 courgettes (largish)
80 g breadcrumbs	3 oz breadcrumbs
6–8 anchovy fillets, chopped	6–8 anchovy fillets, chopped
6–8 black olives, chopped	6–8 black olives, chopped
Oregano; parsley; garlic (to taste)	Oregano; parsley; garlic (to taste)
Wine or milk (to bind breadcrumbs)	Wine or milk (to bind breadcrumbs)
Black pepper	Black pepper
A little olive oil	A little olive oil

Alternative stuffing for courgettes

Replace olives, anchovies and oregano with:

1. Tomatoes; chopped salami or ham; basil.
2. Fried onions; grated cheese; mustard.
3. Mushrooms; chopped chicken livers; paprika.
4. Tomatoes, sardines, fennel.
5. Minced cooked beef; cooked rice; thyme.

Marrow, Hungarian style

If the marrows are young and tender, use them unpeeled, as with the ratatouille. Or, you can peel, de-seed and dice them. Then steam them gently and while they're cooking prepare the sauce. I use a basic béchamel sauce – 75 g (3 oz) of butter and four heaped tablespoons of plain flour to 750 ml ($1\frac{1}{2}$ pt) of milk. But it should be enriched with two beaten egg yolks – add some cooled sauce to the beaten egg, before reheating it gently. Then add one dessertspoonful of chopped dill weed (you can buy it dried). It has a lovely delicate flavour. Also salt and pepper, of course. Drain the marrow pieces very thoroughly, using a plate to press out the excess water, and then shred them a little with a fork. Fold the marrow into the sauce gently. Pile it in an oven dish, and strew the top with a few brown breadcrumbs, to make a crusty surface. Put under the grill until the crumbs are a nice appetising brown. Serve with any simple meat or fish dish. Unlike ratatouille, this isn't a meal on its own, but it is an elegant accompaniment.

Ingredients Serves 4

Metric	*Imperial*
Marrow	Marrow
75 g butter or margarine	3 oz butter or margarine
4 heaped tbsp plain flour	4 heaped tbsp plain flour
750 ml milk	$1\frac{1}{2}$ pt milk
2 egg yolks	2 egg yolks
1 dssp dill weed	1 dssp dill weed
Salt and pepper	Salt and pepper
Brown breadcrumbs	Brown breadcrumbs

Cucumbers

Try this Greek way with cucumber. Chop it, sprinkle it with chopped mint, season with salt and garlic and then dress with plain yoghurt. I make my own yoghurt, from irradiated milk. To one carton of plain yoghurt (and try to get a good Balkan type from a health food shop, though you can use the ordinary kind) add 1.25 litres (2 pt) of UHF treated milk, or sterilized, or home-pasteurized milk (brought to the boil, then left to cool). Put in a warm place until set – about twelve hours in my airing cupboard but it may be more or less in yours. All cupboards vary! After making the first batch, you use the last dollop of it to start the next. Add fruit, nuts, honey and so on for sweet dishes, or use it plain for savoury ones.

Cucumber with tomatoes

Cucumber is also good cooked. Try this very delicate method. You need diced cucumber, chopped skinned tomatoes, chopped onions, seasoning. Sweat the onions in butter and oil until they're transparent. (So many recipes start like that, don't they?) Then add the cucumber and seasoning and go on cooking till the cucumber also goes transparent. Takes about fifteen minutes, maybe more. Then add the chopped tomatoes and go on cooking till the tomato sort of melts. Keep the lid on tightly. This stage takes about fifteen minutes more. Finally add chopped parsley and a little seasoning. Another moment or two to heat the herbs through and it's ready to serve. Great with fish, or any delicate meat, such as veal or chicken.

Ingredients Serves 6

1 large onion, chopped
Butter and oil
Seasoning
1 peeled chopped cucumber
5 large tomatoes, skinned, peeled and chopped
Parsley

Pumpkins

Now to the fancy stuff – pumpkins. They can be terrifyingly huge vegetables. I quailed when I first saw a really big one. No wonder it was a pumpkin the fairy godmother used to make Cinderella's coach. Nothing else is big enough! But fear not, they are tameable creatures. You can either scoop out the flesh, chop it, cook it in the minimum of water and then drain it well to make a purée, or shove it in the oven and bake it till the flesh is soft enough to be scooped out. That's the way Americans do it, I'm told – well, they must have not only enormous ovens but asbestos fingers if they do, because when I did it, I got thoroughly scorched! Whatever method you use, once you've got the purée, the fun begins.

Pumpkin pie

For me, there's nothing to beat an old-fashioned pumpkin pie, Thanksgiving style! One pie shell. I use a *pâté brisée* – the classic imperial 4–2–1 mixture, 4 oz flour, 2 oz butter and 1 egg, or now in metric 125 g flour, 60 g butter and 1 egg. It makes a nice crisp base. Now the filling. To 425 ml ($\frac{3}{4}$ pt) purée, add 180 g (6 oz) brown sugar, or 90 g (3 oz) sugar and the same of black treacle (molasses). The latter really does add a special taste and rich darkness. Then half a teaspoon of cinnamon, a good pinch of nutmeg and cloves and ginger (you'll have to do this according to taste – I like it spicy), the juice and peel of half a lemon and the same of half an orange. (I keep grated peel frozen all the time – very handy). Next, add the yolks of 3 eggs, blending well, and thin it down with a little milk – no more than 150 ml ($\frac{1}{4}$ pt). Finally, blend in the stiffly beaten egg whites lightly and expeditiously. Pile the mixture into the shell, and sprinkle the top with some more peel and spices. Bake for about an hour or so in a hot oven (Regulo 7/220°C/425°F) or till it's brown. It can be eaten hot or cold and goes well with ice cream! You can, by the way, make a soufflé only by adding extra milk to the mixture, and shoving it in a soufflé dish instead of a pie shell and, of course, definitely eat it hot and fluffy, fresh from the oven.

Ingredients Makes 8 good slices

Metric	*Imperial*
Pastry shell:	*Pastry shell:*
125 g flour	4 oz flour
60 g butter	2 oz butter
1 egg	1 egg
Filling:	*Filling:*
425 ml (drained) pumpkin purée	$\frac{3}{4}$ pt (drained) pumpkin purée
180 g brown sugar	6 oz brown sugar
$\frac{1}{2}$ tsp cinnamon	$\frac{1}{2}$ tsp cinnamon
Big pinch of nutmeg; cloves; ginger	Big pinch of nutmeg; cloves; ginger
$\frac{1}{2}$ lemon – juice and peel	$\frac{1}{2}$ lemon – juice and peel
$\frac{1}{2}$ orange – juice and peel	$\frac{1}{2}$ orange – juice and peel
3 eggs, separated	3 eggs, separated
150 ml milk	$\frac{1}{4}$ pt milk

20

Salads

There's no law that says you can't eat salads in the winter. There are some marvellous concoctions that are just as filling as steak and kidney pudding, and much richer in vitamins and minerals. Sometimes people suffer actual vitamin deprivation in wintertime because they don't think of eating raw vegetables.

Winter salad

So let me suggest one of my favourite winter salads. Shred raw cabbage – and the thinner the shreds the nicer. Add shredded carrot, very fine onion rings and a thinly-sliced pepper or two, if possible. Mix them well, and dress them with a handful of capers (or you could use chopped pickled onions). I use this concoction of my own to dress it. I mix paprika, finely-grated parmesan cheese, garlic salt, a few dill seeds, celery seeds and poppy seeds (for crunchiness) and coarsely ground black pepper. These are tossed together in a polythene bag (which is the easiest mixing way I know) and then sprinkled lavishly over the salad vegetables. Then, I add a simple vinaigrette dressing – two parts of olive oil to one part of wine vinegar, and a spoonful of sugar, all shaken up together. Toss the salad, and let it stand for an hour or so in the fridge, and then repeat the spice sprinkling, just before you serve it. This goes very well with hot meat. Try it with gammon or roast pork.

Ingredients

Shredded cabbage
Shredded carrots
Fine onion rings
Sliced pepper
Handful capers

Hot salad

And what about hot salads? Try potatoes or celeriac boiled for half an hour or so, till they're cooked but still firm, cubed while they're hot, and then dressed with a classic mayonnaise which has been spiced with a dollop of mustard, lemon juice (or vinegar if you prefer it), pepper and garlic. You can pretty it up with chopped watercress. Serve it with frankfurters or with grilled gammon steaks.

Ingredients

Potatoes or celeriac
Mayonnaise with mustard
Chopped watercress
Frankfurters

Dress with:
Paprika
Grated parmesan cheese
Garlic salt
Dill seeds
Celery seeds
Poppy seeds
Ground black pepper
Vinaigrette dressing

Chevrier Vert salad

And another favourite hot salad of mine: freshly cooked whole beans (Chevrier Vert are good for this) to which you add chopped radishes and classic oil and vinegar dressing. Then – here's the fancy bit – crumbled crisply-grilled bacon rashers are strewn over the top. This really does taste out of this world.

Ingredients

Chevrier Vert beans
Chopped radishes
Oil and vinegar dressing
Bacon rashers, fried and crumbled

Spinach salad

Since we've got to the bacon bits, why not make a raw salad out of a vegetable most people cook? Tear washed dried spinach into neat pieces, then add a simple vinaigrette dressing – and then add crumbled Stilton cheese and bacon crumbs, and serve it right away, crisp and well dressed. By the way eaten raw like this, spinach is rich in iron. If you cook it, the iron is no good to you any more because cooking changes it into a form in which it can't be used in the body. I always knew Popeye was as stupid as he looked!

Ingredients

Spinach
Vinaigrette dressing
White Stilton cheese, crumbled
Bacon crumbs

Niçoise

Next, here are a few of my favourite salads of the more classic summer type. There is one that can be a main meal – Niçoise. Lots of crisp salad vegetables – lettuce, thinly-sliced onion rings, radishes, pepper strips, watercress, cucumbers (whatever your own tame gardener brings in) – are arranged in a handsome bowl. Now, on top, arrange broken pieces of tuna fish, a handful of olives, quartered hard-boiled eggs, anchovy fillets, and finally, French dressing. There! Crusty French bread and a bottle of plonk, and you've got all heaven on a tray.

Ingredients

Lettuce
Sliced onion rings
Radishes
Pepper strips
Watercress
Cucumbers
Tuna fish
Olives
Hard-boiled eggs, quartered
Anchovy fillets
French dressing

Kohl rabi with dressing

Try shredded kohl rabi with sliced radishes in a French dressing, which is a simple vinaigrette in which a spoonful of made French mustard has been shaken.

Ingredients

Kohl rabi
Radishes
French dressing

Caesar salad dressing

How about a simple green salad with a special dressing? This is my own version of a Caesar salad dressing, but without the raw egg which some people dislike. Into a screw-topped jar put two parts of oil to one part of lemon juice (or wine vinegar), parmesan cheese, chopped spring onion, a crushed clove or two of garlic, dry mustard, sea salt and black pepper, and a little Worcestershire sauce. As ever, quantities to individual taste! Shake this together like mad and pour it over the salad. Mix well, and last of all strew it with croûtons – cubes of bread which have been fried to a golden brown in garlicky oil-and-butter and drained well. Eat at once – it goes soggy if it's left standing.

Ingredients

2 parts oil to 1 part lemon juice
Parmesan cheese
Chopped spring onion
Crushed clove garlic
Dry mustard
Sea salt
Black pepper
Worcestershire sauce

Hungarian cucumber salad

While we're on dressings, try Hungarian cucumber salad. It's the dressing that makes it. Paper-thin slices of cucumber are lightly salted and then marinated in a sweet-and-sour mixture made by pouring 275 ml ($\frac{1}{2}$ pt) of boiling water over one tablespoon of brown sugar, and then adding 275 ml

($\frac{1}{2}$ pt) of wine vinegar. Let the salad stand in the fridge for about an hour before eating it.

Or try this version: thin slices of cucumber (cut 'em lengthways for a change) and thin onion rings are sprinkled with caraway seeds, or anise or dill, or curry powder for a really exotic touch (I've used them all at different times), and then dressed with sour cream. Chill well before serving.

Soured cream is great for any number of salad dressings and so is plain yoghurt – which is less fattening, of course! You can add any number of different spices (paprika, crushed coriander seeds, garlic). Do remember that different herbs make an enormous difference to the basic oil-and-vinegar dressing – I use mint or tarragon or lemon thyme or basil or chervil: just take your pick!

Ingredients

Cucumber (thin slices cut lengthways or into rounds)
Onion rings, if liked

Dressing (1):

Metric	*Imperial*
275 ml boiling water	$\frac{1}{2}$ pt boiling water
1 tbsp brown sugar	1 tbsp brown sugar
275 ml wine vinegar	$\frac{1}{2}$ pt wine vinegar

Dressing (2):
Soured cream
Caraway seeds or anise or dill or curry powder (to taste)

21

Root vegetable recipes

Very earthy, for this chapter. Down among the spuds and turnips and other roots. High-class people used to turn up their noses at these splendid vegetables, probably because they're usually cheap and plentiful and loaded with nutriment. Well, I'm not so high-class, so I appreciate them! They contain lots of carbohydrate, of course (the roots store sugar for the plant's new growth), but they're also rich in vitamins and minerals. Potatoes in particular are rich in vitamin C, and most people in this country get a good deal of their daily requirements from this source. Potatoes are so versatile I'll leave them till last, and start with carrots instead.

Carrots

These are among the aristocrats of vegetables. You can hardly make a soup or stew without them, and you can use them for puddings as well as for savoury dishes (they improve a Christmas pudding remarkably), they're great in salads, and they make super snacks for sweet-toothed kids. In fact, I think they're almost as indispensable as onions, so here's a recipe for using them together.

Glazed carrot and onions

Use either tiny whole carrots, scrubbed but not peeled, or big carrots cut into strips, and tiny onions. Melt a generous dollop of butter in a heavy pan, and then add sugar (about a heaped teaspoonful), salt, pepper and the vegetables. Toss them around in the butter till they're well glazed. Now add a minimum of water, just enough to prevent sticking, and put the lid on very tightly. Let the vegetables simmer slowly until they're tender, about half an hour. If the pan threatens to burn, a hint more boiling water is needed. Sprinkle with chopped parsley to serve. This dish looks as handsome as it tastes.

Ingredients Serves 4

Metric	*Imperial*
450g carrots	1 lb carrots
225g onions	$\frac{1}{2}$ lb onions
50g butter	2 oz butter
1 tsp sugar	1 tsp sugar
Salt and pepper	Salt and pepper
Chopped parsley	Chopped parsley

Kohl rabi

Now let's look at a more exotic root, kohl rabi, which is really a sort of turnip. Just like ordinary turnip, it's delicious cooked to a purée, well drained and buttered, salted and peppered and served up with roast beef. Or you can roast it in pieces, under the beef, just like potatoes or parsnips. Or try it this way.

Young Kohl rabi are parboiled in their skins, whole, then the skin is slipped off (and don't worry if some is left on – it doesn't matter a bit!) and the flesh is sliced thinly. Then arrange the vegetable in layers in a buttered dish, with chopped ham in between the layers. Alternate the layers with a rich cheese sauce. I make this a classic white sauce, adding lots of grated cheese and a dollop of mustard. Finish with a sauce layer, and sprinkle the top with brown breadcrumbs mixed with grated cheese, garnish with a couple of tomato slices, sprinkle with parsley for pretty, and bake in a moderately hot oven (Regulo 6–7/200–220°C/400–425°F) for about half an hour. Very suppery, this. It works just as well with celeriac or turnips or potatoes, by the way. I always add onions when I make it with potatoes, though.

Ingredients Serves 6

Metric	*Imperial*
2 or 3 large kohl rabi	2 or 3 large kohl rabi
125 g chopped ham	$\frac{1}{4}$ lb chopped ham
875 ml cheese sauce	$1\frac{1}{2}$ pt cheese sauce
Breadcrumbs	Breadcrumbs
Tomato slices	Tomato slices
Chopped parsley	Chopped parsley

Salsify and scorzonera

And here is another exotic root, salsify. It is very similar to scorzonera, which the ancients called snake plant because they reckoned it cured snake-bite. There's no evidence it ever did, mind you! I suspect that was a bit of sympathetic magic because it looks so snaky, being long, black and tapery. Since we have no snakes, we'll eat it like salsify, which is sometimes called vegetable oyster, by the way, because it has a faintly fishy taste. It's an acquired taste, I admit – which I have.

I like both salsify and scorzonera best scrubbed lightly – and all the flavour is in the skin, so please *be* light – baked in the oven in foil with butter, after which the skins can be slipped off to serve. The sooner you cook them after they're dug up the better and the sooner you eat them after they're cooked the better. They lose heart very quickly! You can use white sauce if you like, but I think they're best simply with melted butter.

I'm told you can add the buds of scorzonera or salsify flowers to an omelette. You wash them, dry them, fry them till they're brown, and then add them to the egg mixture. Sounds pretty, because the flowers open as they cook. I couldn't try it, though – no flowers available! However, I have fried other vegetable flowers very successfully, notably the bright yellow marrow flower.

Dip them in well-beaten egg, dredge lightly with seasoned flour, and deep fry very quickly till golden brown. Eat at once, and they're lovely with escalopes of veal. And at the price veal is, it deserves a bit of fancy dressing when you serve it!

Turnip tops

Let's return to roots, and to economy. Sometimes you can use the bits that usually get chucked away. For example, turnip tops. Try them Chinese style. Pour boiling water over them to make them softer, and then shred them as fine as you can. Then melt some oil and butter together in a heavy pan, add soy sauce to taste and stir-fry the greens in it for a couple of minutes. Just enough to heat them through, really. Then add some fried nuts – cashews are great, but you can use almonds or even peanuts.

Turnip tops, like dark green cabbage leaves, make good soup. Shred very finely and chop an onion, also very finely. Cook the onion in oil and butter till transparent, then add a half-and-half mixture of chicken stock and milk. Season lightly with marjoram, and last of all, stir in as much shredded greens as necessary to make the soup fairly bulky, but not solid! Eat at once, before the greens can lose their crispness, with bread croûtons tossed on top of each bowl. Filling, nutritious and very, very economical!

Ingredients

Turnip tops	Nuts, fried
Oil and butter	Soy sauce

Silver seakale beet (Swiss chard)

Speaking of leafy tops of vegetables, what about silver seakale beet? You can cook the leaves like spinach, but it's the stalks that I like best. Strip away the midribs from each leaf, and wash them well. Then tie them into loose bundles and poach them. Don't overcook or the ribs will go tough, and lose their flavour. Eat them like asparagus – with melted butter or a white sauce or a cheese sauce, or even a vinaigrette sauce.

Potato latkes

And now to our dear old friends, the spuds. I can get quite lyrical about them! Boil them with mint or fry them raw in butter and nutmeg, or parboil and then fry them with onions, or mash them with cream, or bake them in their jackets – well, you all know that! So here's a different way with them. Potato latkes, and I may tell you that when I made these on the programme, the cameramen and the electricians and the riggers and even the producer were queueing up to get their share – they smell marvellous while they are cooking and taste even better than they smell.

Use grated raw potato, and add grated raw onion – I weep bitter tears when I make this dish, but it's worth it! The potato must be left standing in a colander for about an hour, to let the excess liquid drain out. It will blacken a little of course, but that doesn't matter. Then press the rest of the liquid out, and mix the onion and potato together, with beaten eggs, lots of salt and pepper, and if it's a bit sloppy a little flour. As ever, I can't give too exact quantities because the size of vegetables varies – but for about 1 kg (2 lb) of potatoes and one large onion you'll need two or three eggs. In a heavy pan heat oil till it smokes and then drop in spoonfuls of the mixture. They'll fluff up, but also look ragged. Never mind – that adds to their charm! Turn them and flatten them a little if necessary, and when they are golden brown, drain on kitchen paper and eat hot. They couldn't be more fattening, and couldn't be more delicious!

For a variation, the mixture can be piled into a buttered oven dish and baked in a hot oven (Regulo 7/220°C/425°F) for about forty-five minutes, or till it's firm and golden brown. This way is rather heavier but just as delicious, and makes a change from roast potatoes with the Sunday joint.

Ingredients Makes 1-1½ dozen cakes

Metric	*Imperial*
About 1 kg potatoes, grated	About 2 lb potatoes, grated
1 large onion, grated	1 large onion, grated
Salt	Salt
Pepper	Pepper
2 beaten eggs	2 beaten eggs
Flour	Flour

Borscht

Borscht is the stuff that elderly Russian emigrés cry into while they talk about Ze Old Days Before Ze Revolution. Although it's a soup, you can drink it cold as a summer refresher, as I'll show you.

Let me make one point clear right now. There are as many recipes for borscht as there are elderly Russian emigrés, so I have no doubt umpteen people are going to write me bitter letters saying that my recipe is all wrong, and theirs is all right. Well, hard luck on Russian emigrés. This way is the one I think is nicest and easiest and that's why I'm giving it to you. So here it is.

First, peel the raw beets – and most people tell you never to do that, because it makes 'em bleed. So it does. But we want them to bleed. Then, take 1 kg (2 lb) of your peeled beets and slice them. Put them in a saucepan with 1 litre (2 pt) plain water and one whole onion, and bring to the boil and simmer till the beets are soft. That takes about three-quarters of an hour. Then, cool it and strain it. You can now take the beets and add vinegar and make them into a salad, because the soup has lost interest in them. In fact, at this stage it looks pretty uninteresting itself. It's really like a rather nasty brownish mud. But panic you not – great things are about to happen. Take about 100 ml (4 fl oz) of wine vinegar (personal taste has to guide you on amounts) and four dessertspoons of sugar, and heat the mixture together in a saucepan till the sugar melts. Then add the vinegar and sugar mix to the soup – it goes bright red and clear as a bell as the sugar and vinegar are added.

The next stage is to play with the seasoning. The juice of a lemon will liven it even more. Also, you'll need a little salt and perhaps a hint more sugar or vinegar, depending on your taste.

At this stage, you can chill it, then put it in a glass and serve it with a slice of lemon. Deliciously cool as a summer drink. Or you can serve it hot in a soup bowl over a boiled potato, and garnish it with chopped chives. Some people put the cooked beetroot, cut into matchstick lengths, back in at this stage.

Or you can go on and make a thick soup, which is very sustaining. Beat the yolks of two eggs till smooth, and then add, very slowly or it will curdle, a tablespoon or two of the cooled soup. Return the lot to the soup very, very gently and reheat. If you rush it, you'll get pink scrambled eggs! But if you take your time, you'll get thick pink creamy borscht. Serve it with a dollop of soured cream or, if that seems too rich, low-fat plain yoghurt.

Ingredients Serves 6–8

Metric	*Imperial*
1 kg raw beetroot, peeled and sliced	2 lb raw beetroot, peeled and sliced
1 large whole onion, peeled	1 large whole onion, peeled
1 litre water	2 pt water
100 ml wine vinegar	4 fl oz wine vinegar
4 dssp sugar	4 dssp sugar
Salt	Salt
Juice of a lemon	Juice of a lemon
2 egg yolks to thicken	2 egg yolks to thicken

Serve with sour cream or yoghurt, chives and boiled potato.

22

Tomato and melon recipes

Strange companions you might say, but as they are both fruits grown on the vegetable patch I think I'll get away with it! First the fruit that was called the love apple in England right up to the First World War, and used to be considered mainly a garden ornament – but which is one of the most versatile of vegetable fruits or fruity vegetables, however you like to label them – the tomato. Lots of people don't realize there are as many types of tomato as there are of apple; they all have different flavours, and are all a rich source of vitamins A and C.

I'm going to start with a dish that too many people seem to think comes out of tins – like the town child who proudly boasted to a country cousin that they got their milk from nice hygienic bottles rather than mucky old cows. But you can make it at home very economically and successfully. I'll offer you a basic tomato soup mixture and then tell you what you can do with it – politely, of course.

Basic tomato soup

Start with 1.5 kg (3 lb) of tomatoes. Skin them the easy way – cover them with boiling water, leave them until the skins pop, and then swear as you scald your fingers stripping them off. It's a job I quite like. Now de-seed them, and strain the seeds to get the juice. This is tedious, I know, but it's worth it for the texture of the finished soup. Next, chop the tomatoes and also a large onion. Cook the chopped onion in a little oil and margarine or butter till it's soft and transparent, and then add the tomatoes together with a teaspoonful of sugar, a little salt – not too much yet – and pepper. I don't add herbs at this stage until I know what sort of soup I'm going to make. Leave this to simmer till it's soft and mushy (about half an hour). This is your basic soup.

Ingredients Serves 6

Metric	*Imperial*
1.25–1.5 kg tomatoes, skinned and seeded	3 lb tomatoes, skinned and seeded
1 large onion	1 large onion
1 tsp sugar	1 tsp sugar
Salt and pepper	Salt and pepper
Oil and margarine or butter	Oil and margarine or butter

Cream of tomato soup

Right, let's make first of all that classic, cream of tomato. Put the basic soup in the blender, or you could push it through a sieve – more tedious but just as effective. Then add 250 ml ($\frac{1}{2}$ pt) vegetable stock and 250 ml ($\frac{1}{2}$ pt) milk. Also add seasoning – two teaspoonsful of basil, fresh if possible, or dried, in which case you'll need only one teaspoonful, a bay leaf, extra salt and pepper and a sprinkle of parsley. Cook this together gently – never boil it or it'll curdle – and, last of all, add the juice of half an orange. That brings out the flavour and prevents the occasional bitter aftertaste you can get with tomatoes. Take out the bay leaf and serve the soup with a swirl of cream, sweet or sour.

Ingredients Serves 6

Metric	*Imperial*
Basic tomato soup (see above)	Basic tomato soup (see above)
500 ml half-and-half vegetable stock and milk	1 pt half-and-half vegetable stock and milk
Basil and parsley	Basil and parsley
Juice of half an orange	Juice of half an orange
Cream, sweet or sour	Cream, sweet or sour

Minestrone soup

Now, another sort of tomato soup, again using the soup base, is minestrone. It's really Italian leftovers soup. Add a pint of seasoned vegetable stock, and a good pinch of oregano – a superb herb with tomatoes – and a bay leaf to a 1.5 kg (3 lb) tomato soup base and then chuck in all your leftover cooked vegetables, and scraps of leftover pasta if you have any. Or bits of raw pasta, such as macaroni or broken spaghetti. Cook it together, adjust the seasoning – it may need extra salt – and serve under a layer of parmesan, with a stick of bread. This will serve five or six people, once again depending on how greedy they are.

Tomato and celery soup

Or try adding a clove of crushed garlic, and cooked celery which has been put through the blender to make it thick and smooth. Adjust the texture with extra stock – and milk if you like it rich. For a special summer party, serve ice-cold with a dollop of plain yoghurt or soured cream.

Tomato sauce

Next, I'm going to offer you another all-purpose basic dish which can lead to bigger and better things – this time tomato sauce. And once more you've got to embark on the peeling and chopping lark. No short cuts, I'm afraid! But don't worry about the seeds for this – I quite like the nuttiness of them, so I leave them in. But if you prefer, remove them. Once more you'll need a chopped onion, cooked in oil or butter to a transparent state. As for amounts – that's tricky. It depends on how much you want to make! Try a large onion to every 1.5 kg (3 lb) tomatoes as with the soup base. That should be about right.

Now add the chopped tomatoes, and to every 1.5 kg (3 lb) of these add one dessertspoon of brown sugar. You may prefer it a little sweeter; trial and error has to be the way, I'm afraid. You can also add a crushed clove or two of garlic per 1.5 kg (3 lb) (again, taste has to guide you) and basil, sage and a bay leaf.

Now the patient part. You must cook it for ages. It has to reduce to a thick, dark, fairly solid sauce. Leave the lid off and stand a wooden spoon in it to prevent excess spitting, but be warned. There'll be red splatters all over the stove! There always are but it's worth it because it makes a great sauce. Stir from time to time to prevent burning. If you want to short-cut this stage, and at the same time add fibre to the family diet, you can use bran to thicken your sauce. It won't taste quite so rich this way, so you'll need to adjust the seasoning, adding extra basil and garlic as well as salt and pepper. When it's finished you can freeze it in blocks and it keeps beautifullly.

Ingredients Serves 6

Metric	*Imperial*
25 g oil or butter	1 oz oil or butter
1.25–1.5 kg skinned, chopped tomatoes	3 lb skinned, chopped tomatoes
1 large onion	1 large onion
1 dssp brown sugar	1 dssp brown sugar
Basil; sage; salt; pepper	Basil; sage; salt; pepper
1 clove garlic (optional)	1 clove garlic (optional)
Bay leaf	Bay leaf

Lasagne without pasta

Tomato sauce is superb with vegetables, over chicken or fish, with spaghetti, of course, or you could try this – lasagne without pasta. No, honestly! It's much less fattening than the other kind!

You need courgettes, cooked celery, endive, aubergines – all well drained – and sliced *mozzarella* cheese. Into a lightly oiled dish put a layer of mixed vegetables, and cover with a thick layer of tomato sauce, and then a layer of thinly sliced cheese. And again – repeat all the layers and top with a thicker layer of cheese and strew on it bran or brown breadcrumbs with oregano and basil and salt and pepper. Bake in a medium oven (Regulo 4/180°C/350°F) for about three-quarters of an hour, or until the top is crisp.

You can also serve tomato sauce with egg dishes – try it in an omelette (luscious) – with any sort of fish, or of course as part of a classic pizza. A yeast pastry base (page 156), on which you bake a layer of the sauce, mushrooms, olives, anchovies and *mozzarella* cheese.

Sweet-and-sour sauce

One last idea: add a tablespoon of vinegar per 500 ml (1 pt) of basic tomato sauce and also finely-chopped red and green peppers, a pinch of cloves, a dash of tabasco, chopped pineapple, a teaspoon of soy sauce and a saltspoon of Worcestershire sauce per 500 ml (1 pt) of basic mix, and finally chopped green ginger to taste. Cook together for another half hour and you have a sweet-and-sour sauce that is delectable. Try it with one of the new vegetable proteins that mimic meat – textured vegetable protein it's called. You get it in health food shops.

Melons

Now what about melons? They're a bit like strawberries and raspberries and really beautiful people, aren't they? The less adornment they're given, the better they are. The greatest way with melon, for me, is the one which uses all the perfect fruit. Try decapitating one little melon, lovingly scooping out the seeds, and chopping the flesh. Mix it with strawberries, raspberries and currants and pile it back into the shell. Or just fill the hollow left by removing the seeds with the raspberries and strawberries. Over the top trickle some orange curaçao. And if that isn't the beautiful dish for the beautiful people, I don't know what is!

Melon with prawns

Having said they shouldn't be adorned, I'm now going to suggest ways in which you can vary the simple methods in case your gardener, like ours, takes the bit between his teeth and grows basketsful. Try this. You need a de-seeded, peeled melon (and, by the way, try drying the seeds and then giving them to the children to string into Christmas tree decorations or necklaces. That'll keep them happy for hours!). Cut into bite-sized chunks. Now take a little thin mayonnaise or a carton of soured cream and add a teaspoon of curry powder, or less if it's a strong mixture. You want only a hint of curry flavour – not something that will drop through your chin. Toss into it 125 g ($\frac{1}{4}$ lb) or so of shelled prawns and the melon pieces, and chill thoroughly. Serve it piled in the shell, if you use a pretty little melon.

Melon soup

Next, an Austrian dish – an iced fruit soup. It may not sound too interesting when the weather is cold, but on a hot night on a cool terrace it's something very special!

Peel and de-seed a large melon and grate it. Do it over a big bowl so as not to lose the juice. You need a melon that is really fragrant for this. Stir in two tablespoons of vanilla sugar – that's caster sugar in which you keep a vanilla pod – and let it stand in the fridge for an hour or so. Meanwhile, take the seeds and the trimmings from the melon and put into a saucepan with a litre or so (a couple of pints) of water and boil for half an hour. Then strain it, and add to it 250 g ($\frac{1}{2}$ lb) of sugar, and the juice and rind of a lemon and an orange, and boil for another five minutes. Then thicken it, by adding two tablespoons of cornflour mixed to a thin cream with a little water. This must be cooked for another ten minutes, stirring all the time. Next, put in the grated melon and two teaspoons of grated fresh ginger or half a teaspoon of dried ginger. This has to be refrigerated and served really ice-cold, with a swirl of raspberry syrup in each bowl. Sweet, delicate and delicious.

Ingredients Serves 6

Metric	*Imperial*
1 grated melon	1 grated melon
2 tbsp vanilla sugar	2 tbsp vanilla sugar
1 litre fruit stock (made with seeds and trimmings)	2 pt fruit stock (made with seeds and trimmings)
250 g sugar	$\frac{1}{2}$ lb sugar
Juice and rind of 1 lemon and 1 orange	Juice and rind of 1 lemon and 1 orange
2 tbsp cornflour	2 tbsp cornflour
2 tsp grated fresh ginger, or $\frac{1}{2}$ tsp dried ginger	2 tsp grated fresh ginger, or $\frac{1}{2}$ tsp dried ginger

23

Mixed vegetable recipes

Vegetable soup

I'm going to start this section with a great English soup. Really hearty vegetable soup, which can be a main meal. You'll need celeriac, turnips, onions, carrots and potatoes. Peel if necessary and cut them up into small pieces. First, toss the onions in a little margarine – or you could use beef dripping if you prefer the flavour – until they are soft. Next, add the other chopped vegetables – and make sure the carrots are in neat thick rounds. They'll look pretty when the soup is served. When they are all coated with the fat, top up the pan with a quantity of stock, or you could use water, and put in salt and pepper, and a bunch of celery leaves tied together – you'll want to take that out later, but it adds a great flavour – a *bouquet garni* and salt and pepper. Then leave it! Let it simmer for three or even four hours. In a pressure cooker, of course, it's much quicker.

All the vegetables, apart from the carrot, will then be fairly mushy – especially the celeriac. You could blend it after removing the carrots to maintain their shape, but if it's well enough cooked, all you need do is stir it up briskly. That will create a thick, fairly smooth soup. Adjust the seasoning, return the soup to the stove, and bring it back to the boil.

Ingredients Serves 6

Mixed chopped vegetables
(onions; celeriac; potatoes; turnips; carrots)
Vegetable stock or water
Celery leaves
Bouquet garni
About 25 g (1 oz) fat
Salt and pepper

Cheese dumplings

Next come the trimmings – cheese dumplings. I use 250g ($\frac{1}{2}$lb) self-raising flour, two eggs and 75g (3oz) melted butter or margarine. Add a little salt to the flour, break the eggs into a well in the middle, and then gradually mix with the flour. Mix in 50g (2oz) grated cheese, pepper and a little chopped parsley. Add the melted fat, and then a little water, to get a stiffish dough. Mix well, and leave it to stand for about half an hour, while the soup finishes off its cooking. Just before serving time, drop spoonfuls of the mixture into the soup, and let them bubble up, or you could cook the dumplings separately in a steamer and then add them to the soup. They look lovely. My husband always says this dish reminds him of pretty girls in low-cut dresses! Serve the soup with a big side salad and good brown bread and butter and you've got a meal that is loaded with minerals and vitamins and is also well provided with protein. And it's very economical.

Ingredients Serves 6

Metric	*Imperial*
250g self-raising flour	8oz self-raising flour
2 eggs	2 eggs
75g melted butter or margarine	3oz melted butter or margarine
50g grated cheese	2oz grated cheese
Water to mix	Water to mix
Chopped parsley	Chopped parsley

Mixed pickled vegetables

Now for something a little offbeat in the salad line – pickled salad. You can't keep this for many months, the way you can other pickles, but it will keep up to ten days in a fridge. If anyone can leave it uneaten that long!

You need thinly sliced cucumbers, radishes, spring onions – both green and white parts – baby carrots, celery, peppers and mushrooms. In addition, you'll need pickling vinegar. That's made by heating three tablespoons of brown sugar with 500 ml (1 pt) water till the sugar melts, and then adding 500 ml (1 pt) of wine vinegar and a couple of peppercorns and, if you like it, a few pieces of pickling spice tied in muslin for easy removal. Also, again if you like it, a clove of garlic. Not everyone does, but I do. Allow the mixture to cool, and then take out the spices, and it's ready to use.

Now comes the artistry! Layer the vegetables in a glass jar, sprinkling each later with a little salt, and when your container is full, simply top up with vinegar! Close the lid, and leave it. As I say, this will keep well for ten days. It makes a super relish to go with cheese or cold cuts. Don't be surprised, though, if the radishes lose their colour to the vinegar – it does happen, but it still tastes good! By the way, you can strain and re-use your vinegar mixture at least once more, but go easy on the salt the second time around. You've already used some, remember.

Vegetable pie

If you are over forty, and I for one am not ashamed to admit I am – well preserved, I trust, but no spring chicken! – you may remember Woolton Pie. For younger readers, Lord Woolton was a wartime Food Minister who did a lot to encourage us all to eat vegetables. He gave his name to a vegetable pie of which I am going to offer you my own version. You'll need a collection of every vegetable you can get from your gardener, all cooked and diced. The vegetables, I mean, not the gardener! Potatoes, carrots (don't overcook these by the way: they should be crisp still), onions, sliced beans, peas, corn kernels, turnips, parsnips, celeriac, celery, marrow – again not overcooked. You'll also need pastry, of course, and I like one made of wholemeal flour, with a little bran added. For a large family pie I use 250 g ($\frac{1}{2}$ lb) flour, 50 g (2 oz) bran and 100 g (4 oz) fat – margarine, in this case – with a little milk to mix. Why bran? It gives you a lovely crisp nutty crust, and is also very healthy. The doctors say it does things to your insides that I couldn't possibly discuss in a cookbook but, believe me, it's good!

The next step is to make a thick sauce. I use wholemeal flour again. It gives a heavier sauce than cornflour, but I think nicer. Melt 75 g (3 oz) butter or margarine in a pan, and then stir in the flour, plain by the way, not self-raising, 100 g (4 oz) of it. Stir like mad until it binds, and then very slowly add 750 ml (1½ pt) of milk. If you want to control the fat intake, use skim milk – it's just as good. You can at this stage add an egg if you want to enrich it – use the same method I used for the borscht (see page 181). Or if you are vegetarian and anti-eggs, or not allowed them because of their cholesterol content, use a little soya flour, which is high in protein and very useful. 50 g (2 oz) – mixed with the milk before you add it to the flour-and-fat mixture – is about right. You cook this till it's thick, and then add seasoning. I use a pinch of marjoram, a little garlic, and a hint of nutmeg as well as sea salt and black pepper. Next, fold the vegetables into the sauce. Make sure they're well drained, of course, or you'll make your sauce nasty and thin. Fill the pie-dish – I use a deep brown earthenware one – and then put on the pastry lid. Sprinkle the top with salt, pepper and parsley, and – a fancy touch, this – a little parmesan cheese. Bake in a hot oven (Regulo 7/220°C/425°F) to a crisp brown.

Ingredients Serves 6

Metric	*Imperial*
Mixed cooked vegetables	Mixed cooked vegetables
Pie-crust:	*Pie-crust:*
250 g wholemeal flour	½ lb wholemeal flour
50 g bran	2 oz bran
100 g butter or margarine	4 oz butter or margarine
Sauce:	*Sauce:*
75 g butter or margarine	3 oz butter or margarine
100 g plain wholemeal flour	4 oz plain wholemeal flour
750 ml milk	1½ pt milk
1 egg yolk or 50 g soya flour (optional)	1 egg yolk or 2 oz soya flour (optional)
Seasoning:	*Seasoning:*
Salt and pepper	Salt and pepper
Marjoram	Marjoram
Garlic	Garlic
Nutmeg	Nutmeg

Vegetable-stuffed pancakes

If you want to ring the changes sometimes you can use the same vegetable and sauce mixture but put it into pancakes. Just an extra little idea you might like.

Ingredients Makes 9–12 pancakes

Metric	*Imperial*
250 g wholemeal flour	$\frac{1}{2}$ lb wholemeal flour
4 tbsp oil	4 tbsp oil
2 beaten eggs	2 beaten eggs
Water to mix (about 250 ml)	Water to mix (about $\frac{1}{2}$ pt)
Vegetable pie filling (page 191)	Vegetable pie filling (page 191)
Sauce (page 192)	Sauce (page 192)
Parmesan cheese	Parmesan cheese

Beat the flour into the eggs, add the oil and water to get a thin batter consistency, and leave in the fridge to stand for half an hour. Then fry a thin layer of the mixture in a heavy hot pan. As you cook each pancake keep the ones you have made warm in a clean tea-towel.

Next, fold each pancake in half over the mixed vegetable filling and trickle a little extra sauce over the top, together with a sprinkle of parmesan cheese. Flash under the grill until the sauce and cheese bubble. Eat hot as a supper dish, or a light lunch.

Vegetable curry

Now, to be even more exotic, try a vegetable curry. My Indian friends will tear their hair out with despair, I know, at my method, but it's a very quick and easy one. And it tastes good. So here goes. You need a collection of mixed vegetables – onions, carrots, parsnips, broad beans, potatoes, sliced runner beans, turnip, shredded cabbage and chopped skinned tomatoes. You'll also need some currants and sultanas, a piece of chopped root ginger – the fresh kind – a few chopped nuts, a chopped cooking apple, and a jar of chutney. I use homemade but you could use the bought kind. Seasoning is curry powder – and you have to use whatever sort suits you best. Real experts mix their own from separate spices! But your local Indian grocery will be glad to advise you. Then you will need Worcestershire sauce, the rind and juice of a lemon, tabasco, garlic, and salt and pepper, of course. You'll also need a little vegetable stock and 250 ml ($\frac{1}{2}$ pt) yoghurt. Now, in a large shallow pan – I use one called a wok which I bought at a Chinese shop very cheaply, but you can use a large frying pan – fry the onion first in a little oil. Then add the vegetables, including the tomatoes, and then a little stock, just enough, really, to moisten it.

Now add the chopped apple, the dried fruit, the nuts, the ginger, the lemon juice and rind, and the curry powder. Stir it all up together and then add the jar of chutney. That's a lovely short cut to flavour for curry! Then the tasting starts. Add tabasco and Worcestershire sauce and garlic and salt and pepper until it tastes right. I can't tell you how much – everyone has their own views on this! Last of all, stir in the yoghurt.

Now transfer the whole lot to an oven-to-table dish, and put it in the oven – medium heat (Regulo 4/180°C/350°F) – for about an hour. By then all the vegetables will be cooked through and will have taken on the flavour of the curry sauce.

By the way, if in the cooking the liquid seems too much – sometimes vegetables throw up a lot of natural juice – add a spoonful or two of bran. Thickens deliciously and easily and very healthily!

Ingredients Serves 6–8

Metric	*Imperial*
Chopped mixed vegetables, including skinned tomatoes	Chopped mixed vegetables, including skinned tomatoes
About 250 ml vegetable stock	About $\frac{1}{2}$ pt vegetable stock
About 250 ml plain yoghurt	About $\frac{1}{2}$ pt plain yoghurt
100–125 g currants and sultanas	4–5 oz currants and sultanas
50–100 g chopped nuts (peanuts; hazels; cashews; almonds)	2–4 oz chopped nuts (peanuts; hazels; cashews; almonds)
1 chopped cooking apple	1 chopped cooking apple

Metric	Imperial
About 12 g chopped root ginger	About ½ oz chopped root ginger
Clove of garlic	Clove of garlic
Tabasco sauce	Tabasco sauce
Worcestershire sauce	Worcestershire sauce
Juice and rind of 1 lemon	Juice and rind of 1 lemon
1–2 tbsp curry powder, according to strength and your own taste	1–2 tbsp curry powder, according to strength and your own taste

Lentil dhal

While this is happening, let's prepare the accompaniments, which make curry the exciting meal it is. The obvious companion is rice, but I'm going to do without that. I'm going to use a high protein side dish, since there is no meat or eggs or fish in our curry, though there is the protein of the yoghurt and nuts, of course. But let's add to that with a dhal – lentils, very rich in food value. Take 250 g (½ lb) of lentils, and leave them to soak in cold water for an hour. Meanwhile, chop an onion and a green pepper and cook in a little oil until tender. Then add the drained lentils, together with half a teaspoon of turmeric – the yellow spice – and a teaspoon of salt. Top it up with water, and simmer till the lentils are tender, adding more water as necessary. Cook till it's thick and fairly dry, and then stir in one teaspoon each of dry mustard and powdered coriander. Pile it in a dish and strew the top with chopped fried onions. Keep it hot.

Ingredients Serves 6

Metric	*Imperial*
250 g lentils	½ lb lentils
1 small onion, chopped	1 small onion, chopped
1 small pepper, chopped	1 small pepper, chopped
½ tsp turmeric	½ tsp turmeric
1 tsp ground coriander	1 tsp ground coriander
1 tsp dry mustard	1 tsp dry mustard
1 tsp salt	1 tsp salt
Fried onions for garnish	Fried onions for garnish

Green pea dhal

There's another sort of dhal-type dish you can make with fresh green peas. Cook 750g ($1\frac{1}{2}$lb) of green peas until they are tender, and meanwhile cook a chopped onion and green pepper in a little oil until tender. Take the peas and mash them well, adding a sizeable dollop of butter or margarine. Now the spices, and they're the same: a teaspoon of turmeric and two teaspoons each of powdered coriander and dried mustard. Also a teaspoonful of salt and some pepper. Mix well – and you'll find the pea skins don't break up entirely, but don't worry about that: it makes for a more interesting texture. Pack into a dish and strew the top with fried onions. There – very handsome in colour, making a strong contrast to the curry.

Ingredients Serves 6

Metric	*Imperial*
750g shelled green peas	$1\frac{1}{2}$lb shelled green peas
1 small onion, chopped	1 small onion, chopped
1 small pepper, chopped	1 small pepper, chopped
1 tsp turmeric	1 tsp turmeric
2 tsp ground coriander	2 tsp ground coriander
2 tsp dry mustard	2 tsp dry mustard
1 tsp salt	1 tsp salt
Fried onions for garnish	Fried onions for garnish

Accompaniments

You'll also need some *chatnis* – the word is the one that gave us our chutney – which are cooling and delicious foils to the taste and texture of hot curry. Try my pickled vegetables (page 190), of course, but also try sliced tomatoes and onion rings; finely shredded lettuce and endive; sliced banana sprinkled with lemon juice and coated with desiccated coconut, and that mixture of nutty crispy bits which you can buy in any Indian grocery. Just ask for 'Mixture'!

24

A vegetable banquet

Here is a mini-banquet based entirely on vegetables. And because it's for a gardener (and you're lucky if you see 'em before half past eight!) everything I suggest is the sort of dish that can sit and wait without damage. So the first course is a cold soup.

Cucumber soup

Grate two large cucumbers and one large onion roughly, and then sweat it all in melted butter in a heavy pan. It takes a little while to reduce the vegetables to a mush – it's more like melting them really. Then add a mixture of milk and strong chicken broth. I make my broth the old-fashioned way, with your actual chicken, but a cube will do! Cook the mixture in an open pan slowly (it'll boil over if you rush it!) until the onion is cooked through – a matter of ten to fifteen minutes I find is usually enough. Then put it in the blender for a second or two to get it nice and smooth, and chill it thoroughly in the fridge. Serve it with a dollop of soured cream on top and chopped watercress to garnish.

Ingredients Serves 6

Metric	*Imperial*
2 cucumbers	2 cucumbers
1 large onion	1 large onion
275 ml milk	$\frac{1}{2}$ pt milk
275 ml chicken broth	$\frac{1}{2}$ pt chicken broth
Soured cream	Soured cream
Watercress	Watercress

Aspic tart and vegetable quiche

The second course is really very simple but looks very fancy. In a pre-baked pie shell made of *pâté brisée* (see page 169) I arranged lots of different cooked vegetables in neat patterns. Fried onions, glazed baby carrots, cooked beans, peas, chopped celery – whatever there was available. I made two; for one I used a very well-flavoured aspic to cover the vegetables, made of gelatine, strong chicken stock and sherry. When it set it looked beautiful. A super show-offy party dish! For the other I used an unbaked pie shell, and poured over the top of vegetables (arranged as before) a savoury custard mixture – three eggs beaten into 275 ml (½ pt) milk with a little added cream to be luxurious. I seasoned the top (a little nutmeg, salt and pepper) and baked it in a moderate oven (Regulo 4–5/ 180–190°C/350–375°F) till it was brown and set – about twenty minutes. This dish can be eaten hot or cold.

Ingredients for aspic tart Serves 8

Baked pie shell (*pâté brisée* – see page 169)
Lightly cooked vegetables (onions; baby carrots; beans; peas; celery)

Metric	*Imperial*
Aspic:	*Aspic:*
12-15 g gelatine	½ oz gelatine
550 ml chicken stock	1 pt chicken stock
Sherry to taste	Sherry to taste

Serve cold.

Ingredients for vegetable quiche Serves 8

Unbaked pie shell (*pâté brisée* – see page 169)
Vegetables as for aspic tart

Metric	*Imperial*
3 eggs	3 eggs
275 ml milk	½ pt milk
150 ml cream	¼ pt cream
Salt and pepper to taste	Salt and pepper to taste

Stuffed cabbage

Then I made one of my favourites — stuffed cabbage! Cabbage leaves are carefully removed from the parent plant and put in very hot water for a while to soften them. The stuffing I use is minced beef mixed together with grated onion, seasoned with salt and pepper, garlic and the herb of your choice. I used marjoram. I also added a handful. of uncooked rice and bound the lot together with a beaten egg.

Each leaf is then given a dollop of meat and rice and packed into a neat little parcel, with the corners folded in firmly. Arrange the parcels tidily in an oven dish so that they really are packed tight, and then pour over the top some very concentrated chicken or beef stock. Some people add tomato purée, brown sugar and a tablespoonful of vinegar at this stage, to make the dish sweet and sour. I prefer it this plainer way. Bake the parcels, covered, in a warm to moderate oven (Regulo 3–4/170–180°C/325–350°F) for about one hour or even two, to make sure the rice is cooked through. They're marvellously filling, taste as good as they look, and if you've any left over, they can be frozen very successfully.

Ingredients Serves 6

Metric	*Imperial*
6 large cabbage leaves	6 large cabbage leaves
450 g minced beef	1 lb minced beef
2 onions, grated	2 onions, grated
80 g uncooked rice	3 oz uncooked rice
Salt and pepper	Salt and pepper
Garlic and herbs	Garlic and herbs
1 egg	1 egg
Chicken or beef stock	Chicken or beef stock

Alternative stuffings

1. Breadcrumbs, minced ham and sage.
2. Minced lamb, pearl barley, *bouquet garni*.
3. Minced lamb, lentils and split peas, bay leaf.
4. Minced liver, oatmeal, *herbes de Provence*.

Cooking fruit

25

Freezing tree fruit

Up to now in this book I've been very serious, haven't I? Well, I've had to be – I mean, vegetables are basically serious, aren't they? But once Keith started growing fruit he gave me the chance to be frivolous, and delighted I was about it.

Of course it's important to be sensible as well as have fun with this sort of produce – in fact, to be a bit of a squirrel. Knowing how to store some of the superabundance of goodies your gardener will bring in, if he's as clever as Keith, is important. So, let's start with freezing.

There are purists who turn up their noses at freezing, seeing it as a nasty modern trick, but in fact it's the most ancient preserving method known to mankind, and properly used preserves nutritional value superbly. They once found a million-year-old mammoth frozen solid in the Arctic wastes and the meat was as fresh as the day it had landed there. So what's wrong with freezing your apples and pears? Nothing at all!

Freezing apples

First, apples. These can be frozen either as prepared dishes or in pieces ready to cook, or as a purée ready to use.

To freeze pieces, just peel and core the apples and cut into eighths or quarters. Use only the best fruit for this method – the bashed-up windfall kind are best for purées. Now, if you want to freeze the apples without sugar – healthier really, and vital for dieters – blanch them by plunging them into boiling water for two minutes. This halts enzyme activity which darkens the fruit. Use a metal basket to hold the fruit and a big plastic bowl for the hot water. Then cool the fruit rapidly in iced water, or under the cold tap and drain it well. Pack it in polythene bags and there you are. Or, if you prefer, you can thoroughly chill the freshly-cut pieces, dry them and then sprinkle with plenty of lemon juice instead of using the hot water blanching method. This also prevents the darkening which can make your frozen fruit look very unappetising.

Better still, freeze your apples as a purée. Cook them with the minimum of water and artificial sweetener or sugar, and then pack in polythene bags. I add cinnamon and lemon juice to the purée I want to use for sweet dishes, nothing at all to the batches I want to use as apple sauce. Label them carefully, of course! It's all too easy to forget what you've tucked away in your hoard.

Or, best of all, freeze your apples ready prepared into dishes. Crumbles freeze marvellously. Baked apples do, too. And, of course, apple pies – and a favourite dish of mine, which is chicken with apples. It couldn't be easier.

Chicken and apple casserole

I use a jointed chicken – about 2 kg (4 lb) in weight – and first I gently sauté about 900 g (2 lb) of peeled, cored and quartered apples in a little oil in a frying pan. Then I add a spoonful of flour to thicken it a little, 475 ml ($\frac{3}{4}$ pt) dry cider, a *bouquet garni* and of course salt and pepper and a hint of garlic. I cook it, covered, in the oven in a casserole for about an hour (Regulo 5/190°C/375°F) and then take out the chicken pieces and put them in the freezing container. Next I boil up the apples and the cider in the casserole until the mixture is reduced and thick, taking care not to burn it! I adjust the seasoning and pour the sauce over the chicken and cover it all carefully.

This delicious dish always goes down very well with my family. You'll have no problem with leftovers, I never do.

Ingredients Serves 4–6

Metric	*Imperial*
1 jointed chicken (1.75–2 kg)	1 jointed chicken (approx. 4 lb)
900 g apples, peeled, cored and quartered	2 lb apples, peeled, cored and quartered
Little oil to cook	Little oil to cook
1 tbsp flour	1 tbsp flour
475 ml dry cider	$\frac{3}{4}$ pt dry cider
Bouquet garni; salt; pepper; garlic	*Bouquet garni*; salt; pepper; garlic

Freezing pears

Now to pears. Quite honestly they do not freeze well when raw, but they're great frozen after cooking.

Peel and halve them and take out the cores, and drop them into lightly salted water to prevent darkening. Then make a syrup of 100 g (4 oz) sugar to 250 ml ($\frac{1}{2}$ pt) water – that should be enough for about 1 kg (2 lb) pears. Just heat the sugar and water together till it melts. Don't boil it or it will crystallize! Rinse the pears and then poach them gently in the syrup for about thirty minutes, until they're quite soft. Leave them to cool in the syrup and then pack them in firm containers, coreside downwards. Use crumpled foil on top to make sure the fruit stays under the syrup. Calorific, but lovely. By the way, you can do them whole, if you like the look of them that way, only you'll have to poach them longer and will need deeper packs. And to be really exotic, make your syrup with 100 g (4 oz) sugar to 125 ml ($\frac{1}{4}$ pt) water and 125 ml ($\frac{1}{4}$ pt) red wine.

Freezing plums

Now to plums, and I have to tell you they don't freeze at all well either. The skins tend to toughen and unless you fiddle taking out the stones the fruit ends up tasting very almondy indeed. But if you want to try, then the best way is to halve and stone them, dip them in an acid mixture – the juice of half a lemon added to 500 ml (1 pt) water – and then cook them in a syrup made of 225 g (9 oz) sugar to 500 ml (1 pt) water, which should be enough for about 1 kg (2 lb) plums, weighed unstoned. As soon as the plums are soft – about ten minutes' cooking will do – cool them, and pack into firm containers.

Schwetzentorte

This is one of my favourite cooked plum dishes and it freezes like a dream. You need very well-flavoured plums – Schwetzens are ideal, but you can use others. Make a simple sweet shortcrust pastry using the ingredients listed below. It's a soft, hard-to-handle pastry, but delicious. These quantities are enough for two large tarts, each of which is ample for six people. Bake the case blind in a hot oven (Regulo 7/220°C/425°F) for about ten minutes. I put a piece of foil over the middle, weighed down with a handful of dried beans. This gives a shapely case. Then sprinkle into the case biscuit or sponge-cake crumbs to soak up any excess juice, and arrange the halved stoned plums on it. Pack 'em in tightly to get the maximum flavour. Sprinkle 50 g (2 oz) sugar with a little cinnamon on top together with about 25 g (1 oz) flaked almonds, and bake it in a hot oven (Regulo 7/220°C/425°F) for about forty minutes. After it has cooled, freeze it – covered, of course – and when you want to use it, put it (still frozen) into a hot oven for half an hour. You can eat it hot or cold.

Ingredients Makes 2 tarts, each serving 6

Metric	*Imperial*
Pastry case:	*Pastry case:*
450 g flour	1 lb flour
270 g butter or margarine	9 oz butter or margarine
50 g caster sugar	2 oz caster sugar
1 egg	1 egg
Milk to mix	Milk to mix

Filling:
Biscuit or sponge-cake crumbs
Plums, halved and stoned

Topping:
50 g sugar
Cinnamon to taste
25 g flaked almonds

Filling:
Biscuit or sponge-cake crumbs
Plums, halved and stoned

Topping:
2 oz sugar
Cinnamon to taste
1 oz flaked almonds

26

Freezing soft fruit

Raspberries, gooseberries, black and red currants – their very names are poetical, aren't they? Well, they taste poetical too, and the best way to treat them is to eat them fresh and fast, warm from the sunshine. But if you do get a glut because of an over-active gardener (and our Keith is *very* over-active), then you've got to keep them – and freezing has a lot going for it.

Freezing gooseberries

Let's start with gooseberries. Wash perfect fruit in chilled water and dry them carefully. Wet fruit spoils in the freezer. Beware ice crystals! Now, one method is to pack them dry into polythene bags, and freeze them like that. This is an *unsweetened dry pack* and you can use the fruit for pies when you're ready. Or you can use a syrup pack with a 40 per cent syrup, which is made of 325g (11oz) sugar to 500ml (1pt) water; any heavier and it will make the fruit soggy. Dissolve the sugar in the boiling water, and then chill it thoroughly. I like to add a little lemon juice for flavour and to help preserve the colour. Pack the fruit into firm containers and cover with the syrup, making sure that there's plenty of room for the syrup to expand as it freezes. A piece of foil pushed down over the fruit will make sure it stays covered. If you've got some gooseberries that are a bit bashed and overripe, then cook them to a purée with either sugar or saccharine and freeze like that. Used unsweetened, by the way, gooseberry purée is an excellent sauce for duck. Or, of course, goose.

Freezing raspberries

Raspberries can be treated in the same way, though you can also use a *dry sugar pack.* For that you layer the fruit in a pack with sugar in the ratio of 100g (4oz) sugar to 450g (1lb) fruit, ending with sugar. Or you can mix the sugar and raspberries in a bowl, using a silver spoon to prevent discoloration, and then pack them.

Freezing currants

Currants too can be packed either dry and unsweetened – here's a useful preparation tip: remove the stalks with a fork – or you can use a 40 per cent syrup pack, as I suggested for gooseberries.

Ice cream

One of the nicest ways of preserving soft fruit, of course, has to be in ice cream. And I *mean* ice cream – real fruit, real cream and not a hint of artificial flavouring anywhere. A very pretty one is redcurrant and raspberry. Cook the raspberries and redcurrants together to a purée with a hint of water and, unless you like the nutty crunch of the seeds (as I do!), sieve it through a nylon sieve. Then make a syrup of 300g (10oz) sugar melted in 125ml ($\frac{1}{4}$pt) water, cool it, and add it to the fruit. Next, whip up 250ml ($\frac{1}{2}$pt) double cream lightly and fold that in. Put it all into a sizeable basin and put it in the freezer for a couple of hours, till it's mushy.

Then comes the tedious bit – take it out, and beat it like mad. This breaks up big ice crystals. At this stage, I like to stir in some whole redcurrants and raspberries, to add texture. Stir them well in, to distribute them evenly. Put the mixture into its serving dish and freeze it again. One tip: take it out of the freezer at least an hour before you want to eat it, and put it in the fridge. Otherwise it's like a rock.

Ingredients Serves 6–8

Metric	*Imperial*
675 g raspberries	$1\frac{1}{2}$ lb raspberries
225 g redcurrants	$\frac{1}{2}$ lb redcurrants
300 g sugar	10 oz sugar
125 ml water	$\frac{1}{4}$ pt water
250 ml double cream	$\frac{1}{2}$ pt double cream

Raspberry or blackcurrant sorbet

Much as I like ice cream, my real passion is for sorbets – water ices – with raspberry and blackcurrant as particular favourites. I make them exactly the same way as ice cream, but without the cream. I purée 1 kg (2 lb) fruit – and again you can strain the purée if you want to. Then I melt 450 g (1 lb) sugar in 500 ml (1 pt) water – you may need less sugar for the raspberries if they're extra sweet – chill it and then stir it into the fruit purée. Then, once again, I freeze it in a basin until it is mushy, take it out and beat it again and pack it in its serving dishes, ready for its final freeze. This needs fifteen minutes out of the freezer before serving.

Ingredients Serves 6

Metric	*Imperial*
1 kg raspberries or blackcurrants	2 lb raspberries or blackcurrants
450 g sugar	1 lb sugar
500 ml water	1 pt water

Gooseberry fool

Finally, one of the dishes that put the Great in Great Britain – this is one of the oldest of recipes. Gooseberry fool! Very rich, very fattening, but very delectable. Make a purée of well-flavoured gooseberries. Cook them to a mush in the minimum of water, but don't burn them, and sweeten to taste. You *could* use saccharine, though in medieval England they used honey. Now make a classic custard with five eggs, 500 ml (1 pt) single cream and 75 g (3 oz) sugar. You simply beat the eggs with the sugar, and then stir them gently and *slowly* into the hot cream, using a double boiler. Cook, stirring all the time, until it's thick and smooth. Rushing it will make it lumpy! Flavour the custard with grated lemon rind and – an exotic touch – brandy. Add this to the gooseberry purée – you'll need about 1 litre (2 pt) purée to this quantity of custard – and freeze. Don't ask me how many this is for. I know people who could eat the lot on their own. But I suppose there ought to be enough here for two sessions for six not-too-greedy people.

Ingredients Serves 12

Metric	*Imperial*
Gooseberries (puréed to make 1 litre)	Gooseberries (puréed to make 2 pt)
5 eggs	5 eggs
500 ml single cream	1 pt single cream
75 g sugar	3 oz sugar
Lemon rind and brandy to taste	Lemon rind and brandy to taste

27

Cooking tree fruit

I think the fruits we get from trees are far more versatile than soft fruits, luscious though these are. Here are a few ideas for using good old pears and apples.

Poached pears

I explained earlier how to poach pears for the freezer, but let me just remind you that you simply peel them, and leave them either whole or cut lengthways with the cores scooped out. Then make a light syrup with 100 g (4 oz) to 500 ml (1 pt) water – and to be exotic replace half the water with red wine or cider – and cook the pears in this till they are soft. Then you can reduce the syrup or the red wine sauce by boiling it and serve the pears covered with it.

Ingredients Serves 4

Metric	*Imperial*
4 pears	4 pears
100 g sugar	4 oz sugar
500 ml water or half water/ half red wine or half water/ half cider	1 pt water or half water/ half red wine or half water/ half cider

You could use poached pears to make a classic Pear Condé. This is simply rice pudding, shaped in an individually sized mould with a poached pear nestling in the centre. Pour the red wine sauce over the top and chill well before serving, adding a dollop of whipped cream if neither calories nor cholesterol worry you – but it is just as good without.

Classic Pears Belle Hélène next – I don't know who she was, but her pears are great! They are poached in a syrup flavoured with a vanilla pod (or you could use essence) and served on a bed of vanilla ice cream with hot chocolate sauce on top. Lucky Hélène!

But enough of these Common Market fancifications! Let's try a great British dish made with apples. This really is designed to stick to hungry ribs.

Apple dumplings

You need six medium-sized well-shaped cooking apples. The king of cookers, the Bramley, is my favourite. Make a suet pastry from 200 g (8 oz) self-raising flour, 100–125 g (4–5 oz) shredded suet and water to mix. This makes a firm, slightly sticky dough which you roll out into large squares, big enough to hold one apple. Put the apple – peeled or unpeeled, as you prefer, but definitely cored – on the dough and fill the central hole with raisins, peel or whatever you like in that line. Dates are good; so are a few walnuts. Sprinkle with brown sugar and cinnamon, and then wrap the dough round the apple, completely covering it. Seal the edges with a little water, brush the top with a little milk and some more brown sugar, and bake on a greased sheet in a moderate oven (Regulo 6/200°C/400°F) for about an hour. These can be eaten cold, but hot they are fabulous. Especially with old-fashioned real custard.

Ingredients Serves 6

Metric	*Imperial*
6 medium-sized well-shaped cooking apples	6 medium-sized well-shaped cooking apples
200 g self-raising flour	8 oz self-raising flour
100–125 g shredded suet	4–5 oz shredded suet
Water to mix	Water to mix
Brown sugar; cinnamon; raisins	Brown sugar; cinnamon; raisins

I've made a similar dish with fresh peaches, using a much lighter short pastry, and skinning and stoning the peaches first. Similarly, you can poach peeled, stoned peaches in a light syrup and use them in any of the ways you'd use poached pears. They're very good stuck with cloves, too. Classic Peach Melba, by the way, is a fresh skinned half peach served on vanilla ice cream and covered in fresh raspberry purée. Nellie Melba, who gave her name to this, was not only a great singer; she was some eater.

28

Cooking soft fruit

All the dishes I'm going to offer here can be preserved, either in the freezer or in a bottle, or can be quickly assembled using frozen fruit.

First, one of my family's great favourites – a recipe that's been around for literally centuries. It's very simple and very delectable.

Summer pudding

There are umpteen ways of doing it, but this is mine. Line a pudding basin with crustless white bread. Cook raspberries and blackcurrants and redcurrants and gooseberries – in any ratio you happen to have – for a few minutes in a little water, with sugar added to taste, and cool it. Then pack the fruit into the bread casing with just enough of the juice to soak the bread, but not enough to make it soggy. If the fruit is very juicy, then add another layer of thinly sliced white bread halfway up the bowl to soak it up. This isn't a case for virtuous wholemeal, by the way, it must be white bread. When the basin is full, lid it with more bread and press it under a weighted saucer and over the pudding. A summer pudding takes careful judgement because if you make it too moist the whole thing will collapse, but if you're lucky, it will turn out perfectly shaped and streaked with the rich juices. Sheer heavenly greed on a summer evening, this is! To make it for the freezer, pack it in a foil container and turn out before defrosting is complete.

Ingredients Serves about 6

Thinly sliced white bread
Raspberries/blackcurrants/redcurrants/gooseberries

Gooseberry sauce

Summer pudding is the last course for a dinner – now try this for a first course. Cook young, fairly sour gooseberries to a purée with the minimum of water. Then to each 500 ml (1 pt) purée add 25 g (1 oz) butter – or margarine – which has been made into a roux with white flour. To do that, pound the flour and butter together till smooth. Then add to the hot mixture to be thickened in little knobs. Cook gently till it's really thick, and then season it with grated fresh ginger – about a teaspoonful to 500 ml (1 pt) is usually right. All you need then is a well roasted duck, crisp and well drained of excess fat. Heat the sauce gently, and serve it separately. Very delicious, I promise you. It freezes beautifully, by the way.

Ingredients Serves 6

Metric	*Imperial*
500 ml gooseberry purée	1 pt gooseberry purée
25 g butter or margarine	1 oz butter or margarine
1 tbsp flour	1 tbsp flour
1 tsp fresh grated ginger	1 tsp fresh grated ginger

Raspberry vinegar

Now, how about raspberry vinegar? No, honestly! When I was a child, evacuated to the north of England during the war, a squirt of this used to be put on to ice cream cornets – when you could get them! To make it, all you need is a jar (a Kilner jar is fine, or a large screwtopped jar with the lid lined with a piece of foil) filled with raspberries. (You can use squashy raspberries for this, by the way. It doesn't have to be perfect fruit!) Press them down lightly and then pour over them top quality wine vinegar in which sugar has been dissolved in the ratio of 25 g (1 oz) to 500 ml (1 pt). Leave it for about a month and then strain it and bottle it. It keeps well, in a corked or screwtopped bottle. Use it not only as a sweet-and-sharp thin sauce for ice cream, but also stirred into a glass of hot or cold water as a drink. Refreshing when cold, comforting when hot.

Ingredients

Metric	*Imperial*
Raspberries	Raspberries
25 g sugar	1 oz sugar
500 ml wine vinegar	1 pt wine vinegar

Fire in the snow

And, finally, an exotic idea I've collected in my happy browsings through other people's cookery books. You need three discs of meringue, made by beating egg whites till they are very stiff, adding caster sugar – 50 g (2 oz) per egg white – and then piping the mixture into rounds on an oiled baking sheet. Dry out in a very cool oven (Regulo ½/130°C/250°F) for several hours until crisp and dry. Or you could leave overnight in a really warm airing cupboard. Then you take about 1 kg (2 lb) raspberries and/or redcurrants and you pour over them two or three tablespoons of brandy and sugar to taste. You can use frozen fruit for this, by the way. Leave the fruit till the juices have run. Just before you want to eat your 'Fire in the snow' you build it up, like a castle. On to the first meringue disc you pile the fruit and sugar mixture. Then add the next disc, cover that with fruit and sugar, and put the last meringue disc and the rest of the fruit on top. Pour lightly whipped cream over that and serve immediately.

Ingredients Serves 6

Metric	*Imperial*
3 meringue discs	3 meringue discs
1 kg raspberries and/or redcurrants	2 lb raspberries and/or redcurrants
Brandy and sugar to taste	Brandy and sugar to taste
Whipped cream	Whipped cream

29

All about strawberries

Their season is so short and they taste so perfect just as they come from the plants that it seems absurd to suggest you need other ways of using strawberries, doesn't it? But there are lots of ways to use this delectable fruit so here are some of the recipes my friends and family are particularly fond of.

Strawberry ice cream

Let's start with a splendid ice cream, not too rich and very refreshing. First, mash about 1 kg (2 lb) strawberries to a purée or you can put them in the blender. No need to cook these to make a purée when they're really ripe. Now, melt 300 g (10 oz) sugar in 125 ml ($\frac{1}{4}$ pt) water until it dissolves – a couple of minutes – and let it cool. Stir this into the strawberry purée together with two tablespoons each of orange and lemon juice. Add *either* 500 ml (1 pt) single cream *or* 250 ml ($\frac{1}{2}$ pt) double cream, lightly whipped. Taste to check if it's sweet enough – that depends on the strawberries – and freeze it in a basin for about an hour, until it's all mushy. Take it out, beat it like mad, and then pack into its serving dishes and freeze again. Take it out of the freezer an hour before you want to serve it, or it's too hard. It's a cross between a water ice and an ordinary ice cream and very good.

It's a great success on special occasions.

Ingredients Serves 6

Metric	*Imperial*
1 kg strawberries	2 lb strawberries
300 g sugar	10 oz sugar
125 ml water	$\frac{1}{4}$ pt water
2 tbsp orange juice	2 tbsp orange juice
2 tbsp lemon juice	2 tbsp lemon juice
500 ml single cream or 250 ml double cream	1 pt single cream or $\frac{1}{2}$ pt double cream

Baked Alaska

To be madly exotic you could turn your strawberry ice cream into a Baked Alaska – which is not as difficult as some people think. You need sponge cakes (or you could use madeira cake) soaked in wine at the bottom of an oven-proof dish, and the ice cream, slightly softened, piled on top, leaving about 2.5 cm (1 in.) all round. Put this in the freezer while you get the meringue ready – which is just three egg whites beaten to stiff peaks with 75 g (3 oz) caster sugar. This is a less sweet mixture than the usual meringue. Pile this all over the ice cream and sponge cakes, making sure every atom is covered. It's easiest using a palette knife. Put the whole thing in the freezer where it will keep for three to four months. Take it out of the freezer fifteen minutes before you want to serve it and put it in a hot oven (Regulo 7/220°C/425°F) for fifteen minutes. Then quickly sprinkle it with sugar and pour on a couple of tablespoons of warm brandy and set it alight. Rush it to the table while it's burning. Very spectacular!

Ingredients Serves 6

Metric	*Imperial*
Sponge cakes soaked in wine	Sponge cakes soaked in wine
Ice cream	Ice cream
3 egg whites	3 egg whites
75 g caster sugar	3 oz caster sugar
Brandy to flame	Brandy to flame

Strawberry shortcake

Not so spectacular but very classic is strawberry shortcake. For this you need 150g (6oz) butter or margarine, 125g (5oz) caster sugar, one egg and 250g (9oz) self-raising flour. And, of course, strawberries and whipped cream! Cream the butter and the sugar until fluffy and add the beaten egg and mix well. Now stir in the sieved flour and mix well. A little light kneading won't come amiss – don't be afraid to handle it! Press it out in two greased 18cm (7in.) baking tins and bake in a moderate oven (Regulo 6/200°C/400°F) for about twenty minutes or till golden brown. Cool them well, and then simply pile whipped cream on one disc, cover thickly with sliced strawberries, and another layer of cream, and put the other disc on top. You can add cream and fruit if you want a really mountainous shortcake, or just sprinkle softly with icing sugar.

Ingredients Serves 6

Metric	*Imperial*
Shortcake:	*Shortcake:*
150g butter or margarine	6oz butter or margarine
125g caster sugar	5oz caster sugar
1 egg	1 egg
250g self-raising flour	9oz self-raising flour
Filling:	*Filling:*
Strawberries	Strawberries
Whipped cream	Whipped cream
Icing sugar to decorate	Icing sugar to decorate

So, three lovely ways to eat strawberries – but simply sprinkled with sugar and cream is probably best. Or with a little champagne poured over.

30

Filling the store cupboard

I can't think of anything that looks handsomer or fills a cook's heart with greater pride than a row of her own pots of jams and preserves and pickles. Let's start with an old-fashioned but still popular method of preserving fruits – bottling.

Bottling fruit

With this method fruit is kept edible in a syrup – sugar prevents germs from growing and so making the fruit rot – and also by sterilizing. It's a good method for gooseberries, plums, peaches and apricots. Some people take the stones out of apricots, plums and peaches, but this spoils the shape and may make the bottled fruit disintegrate, so it's better to leave the stones in. Peaches and apricots can be carefully skinned, however. The fruit should be wiped – this is better than washing, which can make it soggy – and then packed into a preserving jar. I use the big ones with glass lids, rubber sealing rings and metal screw closures. Fill the jar to the brim with cold light sugar syrup, made by melting 100 g (4 oz) sugar in 500 ml (1 pt) water. The lighter the syrup the better the fruit looks and the fewer the calories. The rubber band and glass lid are put on the jar, and then the screw top – but not too tightly – to allow for the glass to expand. Next the jar should be put up to its neck in cold water in a very large pan – on a cloth to protect the glass. The water must be brought to the boil slowly and then left to simmer for ten minutes, with the lid on the pan to hold in the steam. The jar can then be taken out – careful: it will be very hot! – and the lid screwed down and the jar left to cool. It sounds easy, but it's undeniably steamy and time-consuming. That's why I prefer freezing.

Making jam

But when it comes to jams – now they *are* fun to do! With jams (also called preserves) it's the sugar alone which prevents spoiling. It used to be said you need 450g (1 lb) sugar per 450g (1 lb) fruit, but there are lots of variations to this rule. Fruits high in pectin, the natural setting substance, need more sugar than fruit. Examples of these are redcurrants and plums. As a general guide 550g ($1\frac{1}{4}$ lb) sugar per 450g (1 lb) of these fruits would be about right.

For low pectin fruits, such as raspberries and sweet cherries, use more fruit than sugar – about 350g (14 oz) sugar per 450g (1 lb) fruit. Also, add the juice of a lemon or some redcurrant juice for extra pectin. You also need water in which to cook the fruit and dissolve the sugar. The less water you use, the richer the jam. I like about 60 ml ($\frac{1}{8}$ pt) per 450g (1 lb) fruit. And no water at all for soft juicy fruits like raspberries or strawberries.

General method

The method is simple. You boil the fruit in the water, if any, in a preserving pan until it's really soft. You can use an ordinary saucepan, but it must be large enough to allow the jam to boil fast. Never fill the pan more than half full, therefore. Then stir in the sugar – I prefer proper preserving sugar which melts fastest – until it's all dissolved. Then, and only then – otherwise the sugar will burn or crystallize – you turn up the heat and boil the jam. And you boil it and boil it till it's ready to set – which is not predictable! If there's any foaming, drop in a knob of butter; that should help to control it.

Meanwhile have all your scrupulously clean jars in a hot oven and your closures ready and waiting. (Closure kits can be bought in any good stationer – they consist of wax discs, film caps, rubber bands and jar labels.) Then, when the jam is ready – and you test this by dropping a bubble of it on to a cold plate and after a few moments gently touching it to see if it's set – you fill the jars to about 2.5 cm (1 in.) of the top and seal fast. You put the wax disc on top of the jam, then dip a circle of film in cold water and stretch it over the hot jar. Fasten in place with a rubber band. If you've done it tightly enough, the film should dry to a concave covering – which proves you've got a good seal. Practice makes perfect – and once you've got the jam-making bug there'll be no holding you.

Pear and lemon jam

A great favourite of mine is pear and lemon jam – the lemon is included because the pears are low in pectin. To make it you peel, core and dice pears, and to every 900 g (2 lb) of the prepared fruit use 250 ml ($\frac{1}{2}$ pt) water. You also need the chopped rinds and juice of two lemons per 900 g (2 lb) pears. Cook the rinds and pears till they are soft, then stir in the sugar till it's dissolved and add the lemon juice. Boil briskly till you've got a set. It's a pale and pretty and very delicately flavoured jam.

If you like unusual flavours and want to experiment, try adding a hint of cloves to peach jam or try adding some finely chopped almonds to a strawberry jam, or crystallized ginger to melon jam. You can play games like that for ever.

Instant raspberry jam

Just to finish off with, here is a jam you can make without any cooking at all! Put 1350 g (3 lb) sugar in the oven to get warm. Then mash up 1350 g (3 lb) raspberries. The next step is to stir the hot sugar into the raspberries till it all dissolves. That is it! Pot it, seal it, and there you are. Not a very stiff jam – but it tastes marvellous! It does get firmer with keeping, if your family lets you keep it. This is one that gets eaten up very quickly.

31

Down among the vines

The first and most obvious thing to do with home-grown grapes is eat them fresh and lovely from the vines. The second obvious thing to do is to make wine. Since there are large numbers of books about wine making, and because it is undeniably a complicated process, I think I'll confine myself here to some other things that can be done with the fruit of the vine.

But first, things you can do with the *leaves* of the vine. Whoever the enterprising Greek was who first thought of taking the big hand-shaped vine leaves and using them to make parcels with delectable fillings, I don't know, but he has more than earned his place in the pantheon of great gourmets of the world. Stuffed vine leaves taste marvellous and are exceedingly economical since they help you use up little bits of this and that hanging about in the fridge. Let's give them their elegant Greek name:

Dolmadaikes

You need four dozen large vine leaves. Use only those that are young and flexible. Toss them into boiling salted water in which a tablespoon of olive oil has been added per litre (2 pt), and boil for three or four minutes. Then take them out and leave them to drain. For the stuffing you can use – well, almost anything! Any leftover meat, especially lamb and beef, but also pork or veal.

Suggested ingredients for stuffing As a main course serves 3
As a starter serves 6

Metric	*Imperial*
1 large onion, finely chopped	1 large onion, finely chopped
2 tbsp olive oil	2 tbsp olive oil
75 g rice, cooked (2–3 cupfuls)	3 oz rice, cooked (2–3 cupfuls)
150 g finely minced, cooked meat	6 oz finely minced, cooked meat
Oregano; salt; pepper; garlic (to taste)	Oregano; salt; pepper; garlic (to taste)

Fry the onion till transparent in two tablespoonfuls olive oil; then add minced meat, cooked rice, and seasoning to taste. Put a spoonful in the middle of each vine leaf, and pack into a tight little parcel. Don't over-fill or they'll burst, but don't be too mean either! Pack the parcels tightly into a fireproof oven dish and then sprinkle with lemon juice and pour over enough tomato juice to come halfway up the sides of the dish. Cover with foil and cook in a medium oven (Regulo 4/180°C/350°F) for half an hour. Or you could pack them into a saucepan, again add the lemon and tomato juices, weigh them down with a plate to keep them from bobbing about and simmer on the top of the stove for half an hour.

Dolmadaïkes can be eaten hot, but are delectable cold. As an *hors d'oeuvre* there is enough here for six adults. As a main course, served with a large green salad to which olives and *fetta* – Greek goat's milk cheese – have been added, a dinner for three. By the way, they're very good stuffed with just the rice mixture *without* the meat.

Cooking grapes

Now to the fruit, the grapes themselves. They can, of course, be frozen. Large hot-house grapes should be skinned and de-pipped and cut in half, and then packed in a foil container in 30 per cent syrup (175 g (7 oz) sugar melted in 500 ml (1 pt) water). But they can be used in other ways as well.

Caramel grapes

Use large sweet grapes and separate into bunches of two or at the most three. Wipe gently to remove any traces of grease. Mix together 200g (8oz) sugar, 25g (1oz) butter, 1 teaspoon vinegar, 1 tablespoon golden syrup, 125ml ($\frac{1}{4}$pt) water and heat slowly in a thick saucepan. When the sugar has melted *and not before*, turn up the heat and boil for five minutes until it is a golden brown colour, or until a little of the mixture dropped into cold water goes hard. Now, holding the grapes carefully by their stalks, dip first into hot water and allow to dry and then into the hot sugar mixture and twirl to get rid of any excess. Put on oiled foil to set.

Ingredients Serves 4

Metric	*Imperial*
40–50 large sweet grapes	40–50 large sweet grapes
200g sugar	8oz sugar
25g butter	1oz butter
1 tsp vinegar	1 tsp vinegar
1 tbsp golden syrup	1 tbsp golden syrup
125ml water	$\frac{1}{4}$pt water

This method is lovely for most fruits by the way, not just grapes, and the obvious whole apples-on-sticks. Try using unpeeled lemon and orange wedges as well. Or large plump cherries. Or small well-flavoured plums, such as Schwetzens.

Grapes are also good in savoury dishes. There is the classic way of serving them with sole fillets, in which skinned, seeded, halved white grapes are added to a poached sole in a béchamel sauce (see page 152), but this recipe is delicious too.

Sweet-and-sour kidneys

Fry an onion in oil until transparent. Add wine vinegar, tomato purée, grated green ginger, honey and pickles. Cook until well mixed, then add the water and bring to a gentle boil. Add the kidneys and simmer, covered, for eight to ten minutes (not too long or they'll go tough). Now add the cornflour and butter mixture little by little, stirring until the mixture thickens and the right consistency is reached – it should be like a thick cream. Season with salt and pepper and add brandy or sherry. Just before serving stir in the grapes and continue to cook until heated through completely. Serve on a bed of rice.

Ingredients Serves 6

Metric	*Imperial*
1 large onion, finely chopped	1 large onion, finely chopped
Olive oil to fry	Olive oil to fry
1 dssp each wine vinegar, tomato purée, grated green ginger	1 dssp each wine vinegar, tomato purée, grated green ginger
1 tbsp honey	1 tbsp honey
2 tbsp mixed vinegar pickles, finely minced	2 tbsp mixed vinegar pickles, finely minced
125 ml cold water	$\frac{1}{4}$ pt cold water
6 lamb's kidneys, skinned, cored, trimmed and cut into pieces	6 lamb's kidneys, skinned, cored, trimmed and cut into pieces
25 g butter mixed to a paste with 50 g cornflour	1 oz butter mixed to a paste with 2 oz cornflour
Salt and pepper	Salt and pepper
1 dssp brandy or sherry	1 dssp brandy or sherry
100 g *red* grapes, skinned, de-seeded and chopped	4 oz *red* grapes, skinned, de-seeded and chopped

That's it then, the pick of my favourite vegetable and fruit recipes. Here's hoping you enjoy them all!

Useful information

Metric weights and measures

Weight

Kilogram (kg): A little less than 2¼ lb
Gram (g): There are one thousand grams in one kilogram
25 g replace 1 oz
100g replace 4 oz
450g replace 1 lb

Liquids

Litre (l): A little more than 1¾ pints (2 pints is usually right for most recipes)
Millilitre (ml): one thousandth of a litre
125 ml replace ¼ pt
250 ml (¼ litre) replace ½ pt
500 ml (½ litre) replace 1 pt

Warning

Quantities given in the metric lists of ingredients in the recipes are not exact equivalents of those in the imperial lists; the recipes will work for either all-metric or all-imperial quantities – do not mix them.

Oven temperature guide

	Electricity °C	°F	*Gas Mark*
Very cool	110	225	¼
	130	250	½
Cool	140	275	1
	150	300	2
Moderate	170	325	3
	180	350	4
Moderately hot	190	375	5
	200	400	6
Hot	220	425	7
	230	450	8
Very hot	240	475	9

Index

Numbers in **bold** type refer to principal mentions of fruit and vegetables.